"Doug and Lynne Seus are the best in the business by far. They deliver what is scripted quickly and efficiently. Whenever I have any animal work, they are always my first call. I greatly admire their dedication to their animals' health, safety and well being as well as their unflagging efforts to protect the environment."

– Arne Schmidt, Producer of *The Great Outdoors, Stay Tuned, Big Fish*

"I love Doug because he's got a wonderful operation ... and he's a perfectionist."

— Robert Redford, Academy Award-Winning Director; Actor in *An Unfinished Life*

"Of all the movie stars I've ever worked with, Bart the Bear is as talented, cooperative, and charismatic as the best of them. He takes no time at all in make-up, never wants to stay in his trailer, and does all his own stunts."

– Ed Zwick, Academy Award-Winning Producer; Director of *Legends of the Fall*

"I worked with Doug and Bart on *An Unfinished Life*. It was such a pleasure to watch them interact – truly inspiring. Doug and his crew were always very organized and prepared. Their awareness and knowledge of the demands of production continually impressed me. We couldn't have done it without them."

– Alan Ladd Jr., Academy Award-Winning Producer; Producer of *An Unfinished Life*

"Doug Seus and Bart, the inseparables, with the greatest admiration for your love and deep understanding of the grizzly and for your crusade to hold and preserve Vital Ground."

– John Craighead, Conservationist, Author, Naturalist, and Researcher

"Doug, Lynne, and your companions, Bart, Bump, and Tank, with great admiration for your dedication to protecting the wonderful bears. I hope your work continues well."'

– George Shaller, Author, Conservationist, and Biologist

"Doug and Lynne, sincere thanks for your open sharing of your love of animals and of life. Experiencing you, Doug, and Bart being boys together was one of life's finest moments in which the line between animal and man faded."

— **Stephen Herrero, Author and Professor Emeritus of Ecology**

"Doug and Lynne are our dear friends who do so much for the wild."

— **David Quammen, Award-Winning Author and Contributing Writer to *National Geographic***

"It's hard to steal a scene from Anthony Hopkins and Alec Baldwin, but Bart the Bear delivers an Oscar-worthy four-legged turn in *The Edge*."

— ***Newsweek*, September 1997**

"Anthony Hopkins, a British actor, director, and producer whose creative collaboration with Bart the Bear goes back to *Legends of the Fall*, has called Bart "the John Wayne of bears.""

— ***The New York Times*, September 1997**

"Appearing opposite Anthony Hopkins and Alec Baldwin in *The Edge*, Bart 'pilfers the picture,' according to the *Los Angeles Times.* The Kodiak grizzly was just a cub when trainers Doug and Lynne Seus bought him from a zoo for $50. He has since made 50-odd movies, TV shows and commercials and is one of the best-paid animals in showbiz."

— ***LIFE magazine*, March 1999**

The GRIZZLIES and US

The Story of Two of the Top Animal Stars of All Time

And

The Great Soul of the Great Bear at the Heart of a Family

© **2024 Lynne Seus**
All rights reserved.

Published by
Wasatch Rocky Mountain Wildlife
Lynneseus@gmail.com
www.bartthebear.com

Cover photo: Doug and Lynne Seus with Bart the Bear.
Photo by Clint Youngreen

Photographs by Lynne or Doug Seus unless otherwise noted.

All profits from the sales of *The Grizzlies and Us* will be donated to
The Vital Ground Foundation, a Montana-based land trust that conserves
and connects habitat for grizzly bears, other wildlife, and people.
The 501(c)(3) charitable nonprofit also works with communities
to prevent conflicts between bears and people.

Copies of this book are available at online bookstores.
To obtain multiple copies, please contact:

The Vital Ground Foundation
30 Fort Missoula Road
Missoula, Montana 59804
406.549.8650 | info@vitalground.org
www.VitalGround.org

No part of this publication may be reproduced, stored in a retrieval
system, or transmitted, in any form or by any means, electronic, mechanical,
photocopying, recording or otherwise, without the written permission
of the author.

ISBN 979-8-9903882-0-8

Printed in the United States of America

For my grizzlies and cubs — all of them.

Contents

Bart the Bear 1

70th Academy Awards 13

Meet, Mate, Marry 21

Kiska, Our First Wild One, or Wolfman Jim and the Gunny Sacks 30

Breaking In, or "Say, What Have You Got in There?" 42

Leap 49

We Move to The Banks of Daniels Creek 58

"Hey, Man, Are You Sure You Know What You're Doing?"................... 64

The Decision 70

Pushing Through 75

Whose Life? 81

River Rapid Romp 90

Five For the Road 95

A Knock at the Door 103

Climbing Out of "Setback Canyon" 111

The Bear 131

The Glory Years 143

Rocket Ride 160

A Sunset and a Sunrise 167

Bart The Bear Tribute 175

Bart the Bear 2, Tank, and Honey-Bump

Muskeg or Movie Sets 178

Grizzlies Growing Up 186

A Grizzly in Middle Earth 192

In His Own Footprints 197

Back Into the Wild 201

The Old Man and the Bear 207

Lions And Tigers And Bears in Downtown Boston and Elsewhere 209

Epilogue: "You Can't Do That!" 218

Postscript 223

Vital Ground 227

Credits 230

Acknowledgment

This book is an extended acknowledgment of all the two-legged and four-legged beings who helped shape and nourish our grizzly family — and the brilliant artists who brought fame to our animals for the benefit of wilderness and wildlife.

I want to give special thanks to my editor, Melanie Seus, the lovely wife of our son Jed and the daughter of my heart. To Faith Youngreen, my granddaughter and my gift, whose beautiful fingers fly across the keyboard as I search for the shift key. And especially to Doug Seus, my husband of over half a century, without whom I never would have known the great soul of the Great Bear. Together, we learned why our lives on this earth mattered.

PREFACE

This is a story that no one else can tell.

That is unless one has over 50 years of singular memories with five grizzly bears, a black bear, wolf packs, cougars, coyotes, eagles, foxes, bobcats, owls, raccoons, deer, a badger named Billy, and a trio of human children.

One would also need to turn back the clock many years to a time we will never see again when grizzly bears in films were real. There were no computer-generated images. The bears' claws and fangs were real. Their breath on the actors' faces was real.

This is the story of Bart the Bear and Bart the Bear 2, considered by many to be the most extraordinary animal actors of all time — and certainly two of the biggest. Bart the Bear was even recommended by Oscar-winning composer Earnest Gold for an Academy Award in the 'Special Achievement' category for his work in The Bear. That performance, and many other accomplishments, helped secure Bart's place in cinematic history.

But, first, and always first, was a family.

"You can't do this," they said. Our families were frightened, and friends thought we were delusional. "Nobody does this. You can't get grizzly bears and turn them into movie stars that will save wilderness and wildlife. You can't do this."

This is the story of how we did it. It is a love story.

Doug Seus and Bart the Bear c. 1997.

Bart the Bear 1

Dan Arden Productions

70th Academy Awards

A cast iron pot of chile verde was simmering on the woodburning stove. It was only 4 p.m., but it was January, and the sun hid behind the south hills that nested our farm at the edge of Utah's majestic Wasatch Mountains. It was time to find Doug for dinner. There was a place 15 feet from the kitchen door that I always checked first: Bart's bear den. The thermometer read 10° below, and a 1,500-pound bear on a bed of sweet hay makes a cozy place for a nap with a snuggle buddy. "The verde smells pretty good," I said as I brushed hay from Doug's coat. As we crunched back through the snow toward the house, we heard the phone ringing. We picked up as a man was leaving a voice message. "This is Gil Cates' office calling from Los Angeles. Gil would like Bart the Bear to be a presenter at this year's Academy Awards." I was just about to say, "That's a good one, Ashtar."

You see, we had a spaced-out friend named Steve, who often wore a wire pyramid hat with crystals attached at "cosmic vortex points." Through them, he channeled Captain Ashtar, an extraterrestrial being from Venus. Steve would call us and leave quirky messages in various dialects, updating us on intergalactic news. Before I could ask what Ashtar had to say, the assistant asked if we would be available at noon the next day for a phone call from Mr. Cates.

At exactly noon, the acclaimed producer of the Oscars called. He explained that the Academy of Motion Picture Arts and Sciences was planning to feature a tribute to animals in film. "Bart the Bear has had significant roles in eleven major films. That makes him a star.

We want him to be a presenter. My assistant will handle the details."

Really? Really! How exciting! How terrifying! The only animal ever to be a presenter at the Academy Awards. Terrifying because … What if … What if?

If we had ever dwelt on the "what ifs," we would never have raised Kodiak cubs in the kitchen. The details were put on paper. We were to leave Utah in early March. Our son, Clint, and our right-hand man, Smitty, would join us to help with the once-in-a-lifetime experience.

By now, we knew the route to Los Angeles well. Head south through Provo Canyon to I-15, stop in Nephi to check for poop, water Bart, grab a coffee, and then enjoy a three-hour stretch of what is left of quiet, beautiful old Utah. Pull off at the second exit in Cedar City for gas and lunch at Dick's Best Burgers and get four additional burgers for Bart. Remove the pickles from his hamburgers and pour his two vanilla milkshakes into his feed pan.

Drop down from the rim of the Great Basin and through the Virgin River Gorge to Mesquite, Nevada. Stop for the night at the Best Western. Call ahead for rooms 131 and 133 that look out on the vacant lot next door with plenty of room for the truck and trailer. Pull in just at dark and make sure no one is watching when we open the trailer door to change the hay, feed, and water. Bart knows his bedtime routine like a child: make your hay into a pillow, eat your carrots, grapes, and chicken first, and save your apples for a midnight snack.

Another 350 miles to go. Rise early to get through Las Vegas by 8 a.m. Then, cross the Mojave and wonder how people ever did it without air-conditioned cars and coolers of ice. The next stop is the Agriculture Inspection Station outside Yermo, California, where we explain that we don't have any produce in the trailer … just a grizzly bear. The inspectors lean further out the station's window. Their overly starched, light brown shirts display the California state flag with its golden grizzly bear insignia. Those were the blond grizzlies that roamed California less than 150 years ago. They survive only on the state flag.

"Pull over to the right," they always say, extremely seriously.

How many permits does it take to prove you have the right to haul a huge grizzly bear across state borders, and that you didn't just go out and catch him that morning in Yellowstone National Park? The red plastic file is four inches thick. I present for inspection a United States Department of Agriculture (USDA) veterinary health certificate, a USDA Animal and Plant Health Inspection Service license, an emergency escape action plan, acquisition papers from the Baltimore Zoo, our Utah Division of Wildlife Resources license, and the California State permit and itinerary. California requires more paperwork than all the rest of the agencies combined. I do believe California is quite convinced it is a separate nation.

"Wow," they say, "Is it really Bart the Bear? Can we see him, please?"

Now we take either Pear Blossom Highway or El Cajon Pass, depending on what part of Los Angeles we are supposed to be in. Sometimes we need to wait in Palmdale until after rush hour. On that trip, our destination was the iconic 1925 Shrine Auditorium, located at Jefferson and Figueroa in the heart of Los Angeles. The old edifice spans six acres, and there, reserved for us, was a generous corner of the parking lot. A big tent had been set up for shade, and Astroturf covered the asphalt. There was a small trailer for us humans to relax in. We roped off our area, and Bart stretched out on the "grass" for a nap. Only green canvas stretched over a chain-link fence separated a 1,500-pound Kodiak bear from one of the busiest intersections in Los Angeles.

On the other side of the fence, shiny-clean luxury cars were bumper-to-bumper. Designer-dressed glitterati walked among a smattering of street people. One of the closest street people, only a few feet from Bart's fence, was a guy in a robe on a box proclaiming to be Jesus. I remember thinking irreverently, "What if he really is Jesus, and everybody just thinks he's crazy?" Just down the street from "Jesus," the production crews were busy laying red carpet and suspending black velvet ropes between silver stanchions in front of the bleachers for the fans, who would start to gather at daybreak.

We were met by a team of Pinkerton detectives. Not just security guards, mind you, Pinkertons. Good looking, 30-to-40-something men in sports shirts and khakis. Most were ex-military, Navy Seal types with Wall Street haircuts and earphones. Every one of them was packing. They were incredibly cool guys.

We met Mr. Cates on the famous Shrine stage. His genuine warmth and kindness put us at ease. He had seen every one of Bart's films and mused that he was the "biggest" star he had ever worked with on the Academy Awards.

He had a sincere love for animals and had produced a segment for the awards ceremony to honor animals in film over the years, including Zamba the MGM lion, Lassie, Rin Tin Tin, Trigger, the Black Stallion, and Bart the Bear. After that segment, Bart would be the surprise presenter of the Oscar for Best Sound. The curtain would open to reveal Bart holding the envelope. We had been rehearsing with a specially designed, oversized envelope because the real envelope would have disappeared between his massive paws.

Production had arranged for us to meet with Dr. Jim Petty, a well-respected Los Angeles veterinarian. He was to stand offstage with a tranquilizer gun, just in case Bart turned into King Kong and rampaged through the glamorous, glorious audience on his way to devour East Los Angeles. That would have been the supreme "cut to commercial" moment. Dr. Petty knew as well as we did that the tranquilizing drug would take at least 20 minutes to work. The look between us said it all. I suppose that the good vet and the tranquilizing gun satisfied some sort of liability.

The rehearsal went perfectly. Only 20 feet from Celine Dion, Bart was entranced as she sang, "My Heart Will Go On."

We went back to the hotel to change. Everyone who could possibly have been seen on stage, or even backstage, had to be formally dressed. I had sent the wardrobe department measurements for Doug, Clint, and Smitty. Wardrobe had the suits perfectly pressed in garment bags tagged with their names. I was left to my own devices.

I found a black, crushed-velvet, empire-waist, floor-length gown for $19.99 at a boutique import shop. I wore my grandmother's Art Deco brooch, earrings, and bracelet. I felt some kind of strange pleasure in knowing that I was the only one at the awards wearing a $20 Bali import dress. I wore my black high heels, but backstage during the show, I wore black tennis shoes, just in case I had to move fast ... after King Kong.

We had to be back at the theater by 6 p.m. sharp. Bart would present around 7:30 p.m. Again, we backed the trailer through the backstage elephant doors to within 40 feet of center stage.

It was a little different than rehearsal. Fifteen or so technicians sat in front of control screens that monitored the stage and famous faces in the audience. Through their headphones, they listened intently to the director telling them what camera to cut to. Robin Williams and Kim Basinger, both Best Supporting Actor winners that night, were standing on their tiptoes, peeking into Bart's trailer to catch a glimpse of his trunk-sized head.

I was pressed tightly against the back of the trailer door singing Bart his favorite songs. "Springtime in the Rockies" and "Puff the Magic Dragon" worked the best. Hearing my voice always calmed him. He knew I would never let anything hurt him.

Then, the countdown-to-live began, with an audience of 10 million worldwide. "Please, Bart," I thought. We led Bart to his mark on center stage, asked him to sit in his "beg-up" position, and put the envelope in his paws.

"Five, four, three, two, one," then the announcer's deep voice as the skyscraper-tall maroon velvet curtain swept back. "Ladies and Gentlemen, Bart the Bear!" The gilded and scarlet velvet theatre had been completely empty during rehearsal. Now, the Moorish Revival chandeliers glinted off sparklingly bejeweled, beautiful people. Some 250 different, exotic perfumes wafted to Bart's nose. Jack Nicholson, with his signature shades, sat in the front row. The audience exploded with applause. Upon this thunder of adoration, Bart dropped the envelope. I mean, he just let go of the damned thing and dropped his tree trunk forelegs to the ground and sat there like a humongous Saint Bernard, looking at all those people clapping

18 | The Grizzlies and Us

Bart presenting the Oscar for Best Sound Editing at the 70th Academy Awards.

for him. I could read Bart's face, "Where in the hell did all these people come from, and why are they cheering for me like that?"

Doug calmly picked up the envelope and gave it back to him. Bart sat back up on his haunches, pressed the oversized envelope tightly between his claws, and sparkled back to the stars — his Oscar moment. Mike Myers took the envelope, skipped nimbly away, and the curtain closed. Bart returned to his trailer, where warm chicken nuggets with honey-mustard sauce waited for him. We took him safely back to his Pinkerton guards.

Doug and I had been given seats in the audience for the rest of the show. As the lights dimmed at the close of intermission, we headed to our seats. A beautiful blond woman in a trailing, azure ball gown was walking in front of us. In the dim light, Doug stepped on her five-foot train of green satin. She jerked backward like a calf lassoed in a rodeo. Doug apologized all over himself. As we continued to our seats, another lasso hit her. He'd done it again! That time, the Hollywood goddess turned around and graciously said, "Perhaps you should go ahead of me, sir." It was Madonna.

Then we had some better luck. We were seated directly behind Matt Damon and Ben Affleck. They looked like boys dressed for their first prom. Their raw nerves were tangible as it came time for the Oscar for Best Screenplay. We could feel the shockwaves of their joy when the young producers' names were announced as the winners for *Good Will Hunting*. Their feet barely touched the ground as they launched out of their seats for the stage. In their acceptance speeches, the prom boys were giddy with delight. At the end of the show, Matt and Ben turned around to us. Oscar in hand, Matt asked, "Do you want to hold him?" Sure we did. How cool to share their moment, a moment we would recall with Matt some 13 years later, on the set of *We Bought a Zoo* where Matt had a touching scene with Bart the Bear 2.

We were invited to the Governor's Ball. We shared a round table with Sigourney Weaver and several famous writers. Dinner was Wolfgang Puck's organic chicken with wild mushrooms. The dessert was little chocolate Oscars painted with some kind of edible gold leaf. Doug bailed early and went back to the hotel. His perfection demons were screaming, "Bart dropped the envelope!" I wasn't about to miss the fanciest shindig of my life.

There were endless bottles of Dom Perignon champagne. I figured it was the only time I was ever going to drink Dom Perignon, so I drank a lot. I ended up rocking out with Sigourney Weaver. She must have stood 6 feet 3 inches in her emerald heels,

Me and Doug at the Academy Awards; it was the one and only time Doug Seus wore a tuxedo.

her chestnut hair piled high on her head, and her pretty little mouth all simmering red. I felt like a "Hobbit in Wonderland" but was so happily full of tiny bubbles that I didn't care. I nursed a headache all the way back to Utah.

Meet, Mate, Marry

In the late '50s, a fair-haired boy with forget-me-not blue eyes chased butterflies and caught frogs on the soft, fern floor of a Pennsylvania hardwood forest. At the same time, a golden-haired little girl with the same blues eyes caught tadpoles and chipmunks between wheat fields on the Nebraska prairie. Serendipity would have them spending three-quarters of their lives together.

My maiden name was Beers, an old Anglo-Saxon word for bear. The Beers family coat of arms shows a bear, claws and teeth bared, with a raven atop a night's helmet. In our family lore, Beers was derived from a medieval name given to a man who had the courage and strength of a bear and was a chieftain of a territory.

The boy's last name was Seus, and his coat of arms identified a person who lived in the small town of Seis, nestled in the soft green hills of southern Tyrol at the base of the Dolomite mountains. The Seus coat of arms is a blazon of dancing swirls and flourishes around a knight's plumed, closed helmet.

Perhaps our heraldry should have been exchanged. Maybe we weren't foreordained to build a shared life around bears, but maybe it wasn't coincidental either.

I was the child of high school sweethearts. In true 1940s tradition, the 19-year-old lovers snuck out their bedroom windows and drove a Ford Model T some 75 miles from Lincoln to Pawnee City, Nebraska, to be married by a justice of the peace they had awakened at midnight.

The young husband enlisted in the U.S. Marine Corps and became a tail gunner on a B-17 in the Pacific Theater. Jack Beers received three purple hearts and was one of two boys in his platoon to return home alive. The early marriage rode the violent, tumbling waves of what would now be recognized as PTSD and ended in divorce in 1955. I learned how to disconnect, survive, and seek shelter. Lifelong skills. I renamed myself Lynne in the seventh grade.

Doug Seus, named after General Douglas MacArthur, was raised in a small neighborhood of cookie-cutter houses arranged on a sheet cut from rolling Pennsylvania farmland. His dad, a square-jawed son of a square-jawed German immigrant family, wore a starched shirt and tie and gleaming patent leather shoes to work every day. In the winter, he wore a tailored overcoat and a fedora. The boy's pretty mother worked at the courthouse. Her beautiful hands were always perfectly manicured, a lovely setting for the fine diamonds of her wedding rings. She held her hands in a way that suggested her lovely oval-shaped nails were made of lead.

Ray and Jean Seus, a handsome World War II vet and town beauty. They were invited to all the right weddings and bridge clubs, and everyone said "Hi" to Ray and Jean Seus. Of course, there were secrets. Ray, an addicted gambler with the brutal temper of his father, had lost the family dry cleaning business to gambling debts. Jean suffered from debilitating depression, the same condition that had put her mother in the hospital for shock treatments. The happiest years of their 52-year marriage were the ones spent raising their boys, Doug and his younger brother, Rick, who lived in the shadow of his brother's burly shoulders. Doug was the captain of the football team and track star whose name is still engraved in the McDowell High School trophy case for the 100-yard dash record. He was voted the "preferred man" of his graduating class and received a full-ride football scholarship to Notre Dame. A faded newspaper clipping shows Jean and Ray beaming with pride and joy beside their son, whose blond crew cut made him the all-American dream.

Two years later, the dream guy hitchhiked home from Notre Dame and marched into an Army recruiting office. The year was 1965. His basic training was at Fort Knox, Kentucky, and his

Doug in paratrooper school c. 1965.

advanced infantry training was at Fort Sill, Oklahoma, where he qualified for Special Forces. Then, on to Fort Benning, Georgia, for airborne training at Smoke Bomb Hill. With silver wings and a green beret, he joined the 82nd Airborne. Although he'd requested orders for Vietnam, his unit deployed to the Dominican Republic. Lost in the headlines about Southeast Asia, Cuban communists were attempting to overthrow the Dominican Republic. His mission: train local government troops in counterinsurgency warfare.

We were 2,000 miles apart, basically on different planets. My mother had answered the door to Mormon missionaries and converted to a religion that would be a comfort and a validation to her for the rest of her life. She packed an old turquoise Nash Rambler and took her three children from Nebraska to Utah with her new 30-something husband. It was heartbreaking to leave my fourth-generation, prairie-born grandmother, but not to leave our disconnected, alcoholic father. It didn't matter much to us or to him. As the prairie rose into the foothills of the Rockies, I knew I was home. Fifteen-year-old girls are ethereal, playful, and whimsical. I was all of those, and I hope to God I have a bit left.

The summer after high school, I was pregnant and married, in that order. At age twenty, I heard my own voice, but could do nothing about it. I was a Mormon wife in good standing. I had a temple recommend from my Bishop that proved my worthiness and obedience to the strict teachings of the church. I truly loved the wholesome values and genuine goodness of the Mormon people. I sat in my white dress on the women's side of the temple, deeply praying for a testimony that would not come. The "still small voice" of my heart chided me, and there was a knot in my throat and a fist in my stomach. My testimony was feigned.

Within a temple that was sacred to the sincere believers who surrounded me, I was living a lie. I did not belong there; I was trespassing, for I did not believe in seer stones, golden plates, or magic glasses, that God was an old man with a white beard, or that Native Americans were Israelites. I confessed these things to the white-shirt, black-tie brethren. My kindly Bishop informed me that I would be blocked in my eternal progression to the Celestial Kingdom, where I could be a queen and a priestess to my husband for eternity and create spirit children for our own planet. Rather, I would be stuck here on Earth in the lower Terrestrial Kingdom. I saw God in everything from the cosmos to the chlorophyll in a leaf, so the Terrestrial Kingdom sounded better to me, and I quietly walked away.

My talent, training, and passion were theater. The heart-pounding magic in the step between curtain and stage was my ecstasy. I moved from one inauthentic life to another. I hid inside the characters I played, perhaps because I didn't know who I was. My relationships with men were love novels in which I starred. The final chapter was always the marriage proposal and profession of everlasting love. Then, I would tragically disappear.

I had returned to Utah from theaters in California, Texas, and Jackson Hole, Wyoming, to deal with my divorce and settle for shared custody of my five-year-old son, Clint. Taken in by my long-suffering mother, I worked for a friend of hers as a restaurant hostess while I was waiting for a court date.

Then Doug Seus walked through the door with some of his college buddies. I showed them to a table. When I handed him the menu, his eyes locked on mine. His friends called him "Charlie

Potato." I could tell he was not from Utah. I was instantly fascinated.

~~~~~~~~~~~~~~~~~~~~

Time of the Lilacs

The lilacs were in tight, green buds when we met. By the time the air was lavender with their potent perfume, we were inseparable. On our first date, Doug took me to Brigham Young University (BYU) to feed a rat to his pet rhinoceros viper. His college roommates had finally had it with the serpent living in his sock drawer, so the viper had been entrusted to the care of the zoology department. Afterward, Doug took me to the first beer bar I had ever set foot in, Harold's, on South Center Street in Provo. From there, he took me home.

Before the time of lilacs was over, I gathered armfuls of the heaviest blooms and put so many in the bathtub that the cool water was covered with their purple heads. I popped in the tub, all naked and pink in the violet, and then called to Doug. There was, and still is, a searing passion and fire between us that has burned through poverty, rage, deceit, and euphoria. The love of legends that will have you lay down your soul. Again and again.

Our first year together is a story unto itself. Neither of us had a roof of our own over our heads. Doug was living in the furnace room of a man-house of "non-standard-keeping" with fellow BYU football players. Fresh out of the service, he had been given a football scholarship. That deal ended when he said "fuck" in the locker room. You might say he just didn't blend in. We slept wherever we could. We spent our last quarter on a hamburger at Joe's Spic and Span Cafe, asked for extra pickles and ketchup, and cut the burger in half. To this day, we have never had separate bank accounts.

I had been separated from my childhood husband for over a year and was awaiting the final divorce decree. I was performing at Robert Redford's outdoor Sundance Summer Theatre, where my soon-to-be ex-husband was the director. I was a good musical comedy actress; he needed a star, and I needed a job. I invited Doug to a performance, which enraged my ex to the point that after the show, he threw me against the stairs behind the theatre and, with his foot on my arm, he damned me to Outer Darkness, the place of spiritual death for Mormons. Out of the pines at the back of the stage, Doug appeared. "She is coming with me," he said. He reached out his hand and I went with him. I didn't look back. I've never looked back.

Flat broke and basically homeless without my mother's shelter, I was offered a job at an equity dinner theater in Kentucky playing the "Unsinkable Molly Brown." I could relate to the unsinkable part. The company sent me a plane ticket. After a couple of paychecks, I sent Doug $75 to help him buy an old Oldsmobile that he drove to Kentucky. The theater housed the cast in private bedrooms with a communal living room and kitchen.

Doug was even less at home in the backstage of the theatre than he had been in the BYU locker room. We spent our days until show time discovering the backwoods around Shelbyville, Kentucky. We met an old, three-toothed farmer named Gino, who lived in an unpainted house without electricity or running water. The house sat in the middle of hundreds of acres of lush bluegrass fields that had belonged to his family for generations. Gino offered us homemade dandelion wine that he had put up in old vodka bottles. He showed us his chickens, cattle, and horse, a magnificent, fine-blooded, coal-black Tennessee Walker named Floyd. The hills around the old house were dappled with ponds. Doug (being Doug) asked Gino if he knew of any bullfrog ponds close by; in the Army, he had learned to like frog legs fried up like chicken. Gino said he would take us down to the best frog pond around, Bill's, on Monday night when the theater was dark.

We arrived at Gino's along about dusk, with flashlights and gigging gear in hand. We climbed into an ancient truck beside Gino and descended winding, ever-sinking dirt roads through the Kentucky backwoods. We came at last to a shanty, and there waiting for us was Bill. The lantern he held above his head cast a circle of light that glinted off the buckles of his overalls and the .22 rifle in his hand. Gino climbed back into his truck, saying he'd come back for us later. "And by the way," he called over his shoulder, "Bill don't talk, he just barks." Then he drove off into the darkness.

With various scenarios, none of them good, playing out in my head, Bill barked once and motioned for us to follow him to his pond. Now, the time-honored way to hunt bullfrogs is to listen for them to croak, then sneak close enough to shine a light in their eyes, which freezes them. Whenever Bill heard the call of a lonely bullfrog, he would do a series of excited barks, rather like the baying of a bloodhound, and have us follow him to the unsuspecting amphibian. It was a new moon, pitch black. Bill's staccato barking pierced the steamy stillness of the backwoods. My job was to carry our wet, heavy victims in a gunnysack. The inner thought of "Where am I, and how did I get here?" does not just occur to demented old people. I was 24 and a long way from the false eyelashes and fishnet stockings of the theater.

A couple of hours later, I breathed easier as I saw the headlights of Gino's truck rumbling back for us. We thanked Bill, who howled a long goodbye to us.

Me as the lead actress at Diamond Lil Theatre c. 1969.

Dr. Glenn Winn

The next morning in the theater's communal kitchen there was an earsplitting scream from the dainty actress who had just poured frog legs from the milk carton where we had stashed them. We had to find an apartment for the rest of the show's run. My strongest memory of the apartment is of Doug standing naked on a chair facing a window air conditioner, with bright pink calamine lotion all over his crotch. He had caught tinea cruris — jock itch — in the frog pond. Revenge of the frogs.

I suppose we knew from the time of lilacs that we would marry, but I recall vividly the moment when Doug officially asked me. We were at the old Robert's Hotel on South University Avenue in Provo; the rooms were $3.50 a night. In Provo, there was a strict unwritten rule about unmarried couples and hotels. So, I had turned a pop-top around to look like a wedding ring so we could get a bed for the night. Over the years, we always smiled when we drove by the Robert's Hotel.

We were married on August 1, 1971, in the South Fork of Provo Canyon. There is a spot a couple of miles from the main road where the narrow canyon widens out into a soft green and yellow meadow. The mountains have always been our cathedrals, and the meadow became our wedding chapel. Some college pals had borrowed lawnmowers to smooth a place in the meadow under a tree where we would marry, dance, and feast on a bright summer's day. We bought 50 pounds of hot dogs, and a friend in Los Angeles who owned a bar sent us 180 bottles of champagne. For a year, I had gathered bits and pieces of antique lace to make myself a "Gone with the Wind" wedding gown of lace, lavender chiffon, and purple ribbons. The colors probably had something to do with lilacs. I asked Doug to wear a white suit. My son, Clint, walked me down the meadow to an 8-track tape playing "My Own True Love." I read Doug some overly passionate vows. When it was his turn to vow, he said, "Okay, me too."

The only family member present was my never-failing mother.

Ray and Jean Seus didn't attend. They didn't think it would last, and besides, I was a divorced, non-Catholic actress with a child. They got used to me over the years, and even came to love me when I presented them with two little Seuses. I came to love them, too.

Doug and I exchanging vows on our wedding day in 1971.

Kiska, Our First Wild One, or Wolfman Jim and the Gunny Sacks

I knew Doug would not be content carrying my suitcases from theater to theater. My two-year college degree was in theater arts, not really a marketable skill. Doug was a combat veteran, which wasn't too marketable either. What would be next for us?

Two of Doug's ever-faithful college buddies were making plans to build a family recreation center off I-405 in the Los Angeles area. They offered us a chance to invest with them. We begged and borrowed $10,000 and moved to Southern California. We found a pocket-size rental house in Pico Rivera, California. The town was lovely, with the clean, orderly houses of generational Hispanic families. Softball-size lavender roses bloomed every month but December. On the tree-lined main street was a local restaurant where Grandma Rita slapped out homemade tortillas and made the best albondigas soup in the world for $2.99 a bowl. The beer was $.50 a glass.

Into that gentle neighborhood, we were to bring a tiny ball of silver-black fur. I wasn't at all dismayed when Doug decided we would get a wolf instead of a dog. I was just happy he was out of his rhinoceros viper and black mamba phase. After some searching, we found an ad in the *Los Angeles Times* that offered wolf pups for sale. We honestly did. We drove to the high desert east of Los Angeles to a ranch owned by a Hungarian family that worked wild animals for films. We picked out a ten-day-old female from a litter of four. On the drive home, I held her tightly on my lap. I have technicolor memories of the tiny, blood-red scratches that covered my face and neck, impressions of her needle-like toenails. I thought her beautiful.

We named her Kiska. Our first wild one. The first glimpse of an improbable dream we didn't even know we had.

Our mint-green stucco cottage had a walled backyard, but we kept Kiska in our bed, snuggled like an infant. We nursed her with baby bottles and cleaned her with soft, warm paper towels as a substitute for her wolf mother's tongue. It didn't work. She was as feral as feral could be. As we tried to wolf-proof our home by successively removing sofa pillows, tablecloths, and house plants, yet another item would be shredded. Yes, Kiska was a slasher.

Doug bottle-feeding and bonding with Kiska, our first wolf.

As Kiska grew, the neighbors cast curious looks and asked curious questions. We explained that she was a very rare breed, some kind of Greenland Eskimo sled dog. We didn't know why her eyes looked like that.

It became quite impossible to open the refrigerator door without Kiska bursting over your back to attack whatever was in sight, usually a milk carton. Once the food was locked in her jaws, the war was on, unless you could substitute a T-bone steak for whatever "prey" she had sunk her fangs into. It was time to move her outside

A tender moment between three-month-old Kiska and me.

and have her inside the house only if she was being a nice girl. The only problem was she was never a nice girl. Once inside, she would lie by the fridge, and the only way to get her back out into the yard was to run the vacuum in her direction. She hated that monster. My good friend, Brenda, a very pretty and well-dressed woman, would not even come in the front door unless the vacuum was at hand, "just in case." She would sit with the vacuum wand across her lap like Darth Vader's sword.

We lived for two years in Southern California. Kiska dug herself a cavernous den under a druidic old apricot tree. I used to love to crawl into the den with her and smell her sweet fur and the damp, black earth.

The family recreation complex turned out well, but it was only a means to an end. I didn't mind Southern California so terribly, as long as we could go to Laguna Canyon and swing from vines and rope bridges at our friend's house that had no doors. It was 1974. Far Out! But the air in Los Angeles was beginning to sting our eyes, and John Denver was singing "Rocky Mountain High" on the radio. So, we loaded an old station wagon with the orange crates, barrels, and cable spools that served as our furniture, plus a few pots and pans, books, and clothes, which was the extent of our stuff. We put

Kiska on top of it all. She promptly ripped out the headliner.

We were off to Utah.

My mother has always taken in anyone who needed a place to stay. At that time, she was a single mom working full time at BYU while raising the last of her four children, my sister Lisa. She opened her door to her married daughter, her not so normal son-in-law, and their 120-pound she-wolf. It was fall, and we started looking for our little farm "somewhere out in the West." Kiska was okay in my mom's backyard until she ate Chantelle, Lisa's pet Angora rabbit, a miniature fluff of beige down — right in front of her. Sorry, Lisa.

After the rabbit episode, we moved Kiska into a pen on a friend's farm not too far from my mom's home. It only took the wild thing two days to learn how to climb the chain-link fence and escape into the Utah countryside. For three days, the quiet, orderly town of Springville had an alert: WOLF AT LARGE. DO NOT LET CHILDREN OUTSIDE ALONE.

We searched irrigation ditches, hay fields, backyards, and parking lots for Kiska. We had offered a $50 reward. That was a lot of money when a hamburger cost a quarter. Finally, we received a call from a farmer who had cornered a snarling Kiska in the back of his barn. He took the money and gladly gave us back our wolf as he mumbled under his breath, "We just got rid of them goddamned sonsabitches."

The next day, there was a picture on the front page of the *Provo Daily Herald* of Doug, Kiska, and me reunited. "Tame Wolf Strays; Returned to Owners," said the headline. Doug had a choke hold on her neck.

We spent the winter at mom's, looking every day for a place of our own. We came close to buying a couple of old farms on the bustling Wasatch Front, but the Heber Valley was calling to us 1,000 feet higher into the mountains, with only a single stoplight on Main Street. We drove at least one real estate agent crazy — "too expensive, too run down, too big, too little, not enough acreage, too close to town." We finally started knocking on the doors of houses that looked right to us. Doug had long hair and a mountain man

Tame Wolf Strays; Returned to Owners

By JESSIE NILSON

SPRINGVILLE — A tame timberline wolf which strayed away from the Bess Freeman residence in Springville Friday was recaptured this morning when she tried to move in with a group of dogs belonging to Jim Hall here.

The wolf was brought to Springville with Mr. and Mrs. Doug Seus of California. The Seuses were in Springville with her mother, Mrs. Freeman, to attend a wedding, and they brought the wolf with them.

The Seuses have had the wolf, Kiska, since she was 17 days old, and have loved and cared for her since. Mr. Seus is doing research on the social nature of the endangered species of timber wolf, of which Kiska is a sub-species.

Mr. and Mrs. Delos Nilsen of Palmyra were confronted by Kiska Sunday evening shortly before 9 on the road west of Springville. They learned that Kiska was missing, and called the owners, who spent much of the night looking for her in the area. However, it was not until this morning that Kiska was found at the Halls. Jim said that Kiska was trying to move in with his other animals.

Mr. Seus claims that wolves are not vicious animals, and that there has never been a documented case of one's attacking a human being. He says that dogs are born with fierceness, but can be easily tamed.

Wolves, on the other hand, are tenderhearted creatures in the first place. They like to be around people, but are shy by nature.

The Seuses thanked everyone involved in the search.

to give the voters the options of having partial fare or other options, he said.

Two measures which were defeated were the bill to raise the county's bonding limit to five per cent, one of the major reasons for calling the special session, and the bill to allow the consolidation committee in Salt Lake County to be recommissioned to make minor changes.

Mr. Nielson said the constitutional amendment regarding bonding limits was defeated by legislators who felt it was putting the cart before the horse and could be re-introduced when and if consolidation is accepted.

Lobby Threat

He also pointed out that many people felt recommissioning the consolidation committee would allow it to be come a lobbying effort for consolidation, operating at the taxpayers' expense.

Mr. Nielson said he had predicted the bonding measure would be defeated because a similar, and weaker, bill was defeated in the House in

(Continued on Page 5)

DOUG AND LYNNE SEUS enjoy reunion with pet timberline wolf in Springville. The animal, which they've had since she was 17 days old, strayed away Friday but was returned to the Seuses this morning after trying to move in with a group of dogs belonging to Jim Hall. (Photo by Oneita Sumsion)

The Provo Daily Herald Newspaper article about the return of Kiska.

beard; I wore crocheted tops and jeans and boots. We did not exactly look like locals. Many of those doors shut quickly. Then we stopped at a 1919 farmhouse nestled against the south hills of the valley — a mountain brook wound through the acreage.

The door opened to the face of a hardscrabble farmer. We asked the question, "Is there a chance you might be interested in ever selling?" He studied us for a moment, then said, "We will be moving back to Idaho when my last girl graduates from high school." We knew it was the perfect place for us, but his daughter was only a junior. We had a year and a half wait before we could move into our little farmhouse on the banks of Daniels Creek.

In the meantime, there was a new, split-level home for sale in the middle of the valley on Center Creek. The son of a pioneering Heber family had built the house a few years before. It had just come up for sale in a divorce settlement. We reasoned that if we could come up with the $300-a-month mortgage payment, we might be able to resell it later for a profit. It scared us, but we both had day jobs, and that became the plan.

The neighbors watched us as we built our wolf run. They were warm and friendly, but the word going around was truly spoken when the five-year-old child next door called over the fence, "Doug, my dad says you is a hippie." We were warmly welcomed, anyway. So, with a place of our own at last, it was just natural we wanted to expand the family. Kiska needed a mate, and we were trying to make a human baby.

~~~~~~~~~~~~~~~~~~~~~~

A rancher across the back field told us about an old government trapper who lived about 40 miles away in the town of Lehi. He said that the seasoned trapper was known for denning and keeping several of the "vermin" species he was supposed to have trapped and killed for stockmen in the West Desert. We arranged to meet Wolfman Jim. He was tall, raw-boned, bent, and grizzled, and he dressed in overalls that smelled of decay and bobcat urine. The strange divot in his forehead, we learned later, was from a failed suicide attempt over a broken marriage. Locally, he was called "Old Bulletproof," instead of Wolfman. Jim's family homestead was on the outskirts of a small agrarian town between Provo and Salt Lake. Nothing on the old farm had been changed or thrown away since his parents died, probably in the late '50s. Between the driveway and the front door was an obstacle course of rotting tires, broken tools, tractor parts, rusted milk cans, shattered window frames, chicken shit, and lots of cats, most of them alive.

Jim asked us in for a cup of coffee. The interior of the house was most likely just as it had been during Jim's childhood. His mother had had a fancy for sweet potato plants, supported by toothpicks, in Mason jars full of murky water. His sister, Margarette, continued the tradition; sweet potato vines crawled about the kitchen, including the only window, giving the rooms a peculiar shade of green light.

With coffee and evaporated milk in chipped cups, he led us into the front room, where worn, overstuffed chairs sat on either side of the potbelly wood stove. Once Mom's and Dad's, these chairs were now Margarette's and Jim's. Doug and I sat on the edge of an old sofa layered with various greasy quilts to cover what was left of the original fabric. Jim spun yarns of his life in the hills looking for critters. Then he took us out back to see his animals. Concrete slabs supported chain-link cages that held coyotes, an ancient black bear, raccoons, badgers, bobcats, and three cream-colored wolves. He said the wolves were the last of Utah's buffalo wolves, and that he had denned them in the West Desert years before. I'm sure they should have become a source of DNA for study because there were not supposed to be any buffalo wolves left in Utah. In fact, there were not supposed to be wolves of *any* kind in Utah outside a zoo. Sadly, no one seemed to care.

Jim was eager to show us his new raccoon that someone had just given him, "a pure pet" named Rocky. We stepped into a lean-to shed where Rocky paced in his walk-in cage. "Come on in and pet him; he's as gentle as a kitten," Jim said. The glittering obsidian eyes behind the mask warned me, but I followed Jim and Doug into the cage. Rocky tiptoed over to sniff my shoes and proceeded to climb my leg like a tree trunk, attacking bite by bite as he made his way to my butt. I screamed. Jim pulled the crazed creature off my leg, receiving a nasty bite to his hand. He held "pure pet" Rocky down as Doug and I escaped the cage. My lesson was to trust my senses. This lesson was renewed every time I rebandaged my leg, which looked like I had been attacked by an ice pick murderer.

~~~~~~~~~~~~~~~~~~~~~~~

We saw a lot of Wolfman Jim that fall. He took us deep into the Cedar Hills of the West Desert, where he had spent long years denning varmints for local sheep ranchers. It was indeed magical to see cougar prints in the soft red earth between the cedars. The hills seemed lonely and quiet until a glint of sunlight on a piece of chipped flint spoke great stories. The sound of women laughing, babies crying, and Native American flutes echoed hauntingly among the junipers.

Me and Wiley the coyote, one of the "varmints" from *Wolfman Jim*.

Later that autumn, Jim phoned to tell us someone had dropped off a wolf they could no longer care for at his front door. He said he was named Nero. With the scars on my legs still glowing an interesting shade of purple, we drove down to see Nero. He was huge. There were no breeding records, of course, but the fiery yellow eyes, gnarly snowshoe feet, and plump tail that dropped straight down to his hocks showed pure wolf. He huddled shyly at the back of his pen until I knelt down and whispered his name. Then he crept slowly forward and rubbed his tawny, black-tinged mane on my fingers. He was coming home with us.

Kiska watched with steely eyes as we led Nero from our truck to the wolf run. We walked the big male outside the perimeter of the run several times so he could sniff and pee and sniff and pee until he ran out of pee. All the while, Kiska sat on her den mound like a queen, never taking her eyes off him. When we opened the gate and brought him inside, she charged off her throne, knocking him over and biting him hard on the chin. Then she turned around and exposed her girly parts to him. It was love at first sight and the beginning of our wolf pack.

That winter, Doug was working at a sawmill in the Kamas Valley, and I was working for Sunn Classic Pictures as a script coordinator for a film called *In Search of Noah's Ark*. There was a professional movie-animal company from Los Angeles on the project. Wow! If only we could ever do such a thing! The dream, and the classic catch-22: how do you get a job without a credit, and how do you get a credit without a job? Our elusive dream.

As winter changed to early spring, we had some changes, too. The movie I was working on was finished, and Doug found a higher-paying job driving a cement truck. The new job paid $3.75 an hour, $.75 an hour more than the sawmill. I was looking for a new job, and one came to me. It was Easter, the time of rebirth. There were lambs, calves, and foals in the fields, and the wild things were also having their young. As Jim denned varmints for the ranchers, he was supposed to put them in gunnysacks and drown them. Instead, the gunnysacks arrived at our door, and out tumbled skunks, coyotes, grey foxes, a badger, and a bobcat kitten. We obtained a Wildlife Rehabilitator License from the Utah Department of Wildlife Resources. One morning, park rangers brought us two tiny, orphaned mule deer fawns, no bigger than whippets.

In those days, paper towels still came in huge cardboard boxes from the general store. Those boxes served as our pens. The local sawmill gave us all the sawdust we could use. In exchange for a peek at the babies, the neighbors brought us stacks and stacks of newspapers. Along with five big buckets, lots of rags, and mops, I was ready. Baby bottles, eyedroppers, canned milk, and homemade chicken broth in Mason jars lined our kitchen counter for months.

Newborn wild animals of any species must imprint on humans if they are going to live in the human world. As their eyes opened, we fed these tiny ones from baby bottles, all the while cuddling, petting, and singing them to sleep with gentle songs to accustom them to the human voice. For these wild babies, the first impression of humans would be the smell, gentle touch, sight, and sound of humans, as well as the taste of cream and chicken broth in their nursing bottles.

Among those babies were six tiny striped skunks. One night, the little stinkers escaped from their cardboard box. Being nocturnal by nature, skunks like dark, cozy places. They headed straight for the heat register and down into the house's heating ducts. They seemed to be right at home. Too young to have been descented, and hog fat from their diet of whipping cream and chicken broth, they ran around the heating duct system like hamsters on a wheel.

Now, late March in the Rockies can still be cold and snowy, so for over a week, we wore wool sweaters, heavy socks, and hats pulled down over our ears. For God's sake, we couldn't turn on the furnace lest the poor darlings get cooked. Besides, if that happened, we would have to tear up the floorboards to get to their nasty little bodies. No tidbit I held above the registers presented a greater temptation than the joy of running free in the ductwork. One rainy afternoon, while making a peanut butter and jelly sandwich, I remembered that I had not tried peanut butter. I held the sandwich over the floor register. There were 12 shiny, black-bead eyes looking up at me. One by one, they crawled upward. Gooey bread in one hand, I grabbed their bristly, stinky mustelid, asses with the other, receiving needle bites to my fingers in the process. The bitty polecats were no worse for their sojourn in furnace land.

We had named the badger cub Billy. He was trained to a litter box and liked to hang out in the house with us. One unusual feature of the Center Creek house was a very large bathroom on the main level. The former owners had chosen black porcelain for the tub and sink and deep-green marble for flooring. Billy decided that the cool, dark space between the back of the toilet and the wall was a terrific spot for his den. Most of the time, he would lie on his back with his stubby black paws and white claws up in the air, like a soft, grey sofa pillow with legs. It was fun to reach down and rub his tummy while you were seated on the pot ... that is, if he knew you. Strangers' ankles were fair game. I'm not sure why Doug and I thought it was so funny not to mention that there was a badger behind the toilet. We would linger at the end of the hallway and wait for visitors to appear wide-eyed and white-faced with their pants down around their ankles like two-year-olds. I still think it's funny.

Kiska and Nero presented us with three charcoal-colored wolf pups. The proud parents had dug a commodious den, even bigger than the one Kiska had dug for herself in Los Angeles. The new mother allowed us to enter the cavern as her mate watched from the top of the mound. The glossy little minks hummed in contentment. We knew we had to bottle-raise them, but how could we take Kiska's babies from her when she trusted us to lie with her in her den and pick them up?

I had an idea. I checked with the local Humane Society in Salt Lake City. Luckily, there was a stray collie mix with five newborn pups. We adopted three of them. The next day, we waited for Kiska to come out of the den to feed and have her daily brawl with Nero. While she was distracted, Doug smuggled the collie pups into his jacket, crawled into the den, and made the switch. As we crept back to the gate, Nero's and Kiska's eyes narrowed, and they charged back into the den. Only Nero emerged. Doug continued to the gate with the wolf pups. I could not stand not knowing what was happening, so I crawled back into the den. Kiska was standing over the pups, sniffing them intently. Would she kill them? Would she kill me? She continued to examine them, then gave me a really evil, knowing look and lay down to let them nurse.

Later that spring, the neighbors would be so proud of their collie pups raised by wolves.

As spring turned into summer, the wild babies turned into youngsters, and we moved them outside into various pens. I stayed close by as I planted a garden of beets, onions, potatoes, beans, and squash. I learned how to make a great batch of chicken and dumplings from the chicken necks we bought for a nickel a pound. Doug had been able to hunt and harvest a fine bull elk that fall, so our freezer was full of the strong, red meat. Most every meal was elk steak, fried potatoes, pickled beets, and biscuits. We had to go to the grocery store once in a while for beer and coffee. An orange was a rare treat. I learned to savor every bite.

Then three life-changing things happened: we got pregnant; we got our first animal movie; and we got Kodiak bear cubs — one of them we named Bart.

Breaking In, or "Say, What Have You Got in there?"

The plan and path were clear before us. We knew that if we were to follow our dream, our future movie animals would have to be socialized to be comfortable in strange places around strange people. The wolves watched rodeos. The coyotes and bobcats went to the Future Farmers of America and science classes at the local high school. The foxes and porcupines visited Boy Scout camps. Billy the Badger went bowling with us, and the raccoons went to the city park playground to share the swings and slides with the town's children.

One rainy day, while running errands, I took along a wicker picnic basket full of baby skunks. The local hardware store was in a remodeled 1930s house with bookcases for shelves and squeaky, shiplap wood floors. I was waiting with a paper bag full of five-penny nails at the cash register. I had the basket over my arm and the bag of nails in my hand. As I was fishing a dollar out of my pocket, the little "Poohs," as we called them, were poking their shiny black noses out of the wicker basket. "Say, what have you got in there?" asked the stranger behind me. I explained that I was socializing baby skunks and getting them used to strange places because we hoped to use them in movies and such. He said that his name was Bill and he was the prop master for a movie that was getting ready to shoot above Sundance in Provo Canyon. He turned his card over and wrote the phone number of the production office on the back. "Why don't you give them a call? There are all kinds of animals in the script." I thanked him kindly, trying really hard to act cool; then I

Me with the little "stinkers" who helped land us our first movie job.

raced madly home and ran squealing into the house. "Doug, you won't believe this! Seriously, you won't BELIEVE IT!"

The production office had just opened in Provo. The film was *Baker's Hawk*, a major motion picture with major stars. We were still driving the Oldsmobile that we had bought for $75. It was still running ... kind of. It belched blue smoke that matched its one blue fender. The rest of it was a rusty white. We parked four blocks away from the production office, reasoning that if anyone saw us driving that old wreck of a car, we would never get the big bucks we were planning to ask for. The producer was from New York, loud, brash, and tough, but he took an instant liking to Doug and also to the fact that we could supply the red-tailed hawk, the deer, the skunks, the porcupine, the coyote, the wolves, the raccoon, the badger, and the bobcat. Oh, and yes, of course, we would also be the nighttime security guards. All for the tidy sum of $6,000 for the eight-week shoot. The day we signed the contract, I found out I was pregnant.

The movie was a coming-of-age story centered on a boy who rescues a wounded red-tailed hawk, helped by a kindly hermit living in a remote cabin high up in the mountains. The gentle recluse is surrounded by all kinds of wild creatures that he had rescued and nurtured. The location was just above Robert Redford's home; the iconic movie *Jeremiah Johnson* had been filmed at the same spot just a few years before. Mount Timpanogos defined the skyline.

We arrived on set and met the cast. Burl Ives, America's Troubadour, "Big Daddy," Oscar-winner for *The Big Country*, played the kindly hermit. He was a squeezable teddy bear of a man. Lee Montgomery, who had starred in Ben, the all-time classic rat movie, played the hero boy. Clint Walker, of *Cheyenne* fame, played the dad — all 6 feet 5 inches of him. Into the accomplished and worthy cast stumbled two first-time "professional" animal trainers and their family of wild things.

Our down payment bought us a used Dodge pickup truck. We borrowed a friend's camper shell and moved the animals and ourselves to the backside of Timpanogos for eight weeks. We put up makeshift pens for the animals. They were like little kids on a camping trip. The two fawns loved scampering through the meadow of wildflowers, and our raccoon, Mizzer, quickly decided he would live in the aspen tree that shaded our camper. We looked like a little movie unto itself.

At the time, we did not have a red-tailed hawk, but we had often accompanied our friend Richard to the Utah King Frederick Falconry meets, along with Wilma, his female red-tailed hawk. The falconry club delighted in re-creating the medieval falconry of King Fredrick, down to replicas of the falconer's gloves and the hoods

Burl Ives with our hawk Wilma on the set of *Baker's Hawk*.

Yukon the wolf, Clint Walker, and me on the set of *Baker's Hawk*.

and leg jesses used for the birds. Wilma would circle high overhead until called down with a whistle down for a juicy piece of red meat held in a carefully gloved hand. Wilma would be *Baker's hawk*.

Now, raptors are beautifully designed predators, but in my opinion, they have no need for mammalian affection. We would check Wilma's weight at the start of each day, and once she had her measured ounces of raw beef heart, she was done for the day. Occasionally, though, we would go on a wild goose, well, a wild hawk chase, and have to climb some ridiculously high tree, where she would reluctantly allow herself to be caught by her jesses and accept her hood.

We learned by bits and pieces of on-the-job training and embarrassment. The director had a brilliant thought! Wouldn't it be great to have an ending shot of the fawns walking off into the sunset beside a magnificent buck, with the hawk flying overhead? The shot wasn't in the script or in our deal, but the producer said an extra hundred dollars or so was available if we could pull it off. We were on it! We only had the two orphan fawns in our mixed bag of four-legged critters, but our friend Steve was a curator at the Tracey Aviary located in Salt Lake City. The aviary exhibited mostly birds but also had an exhibit of Utah mule deer. The monarch of the small herd was a splendid six-point buck. The studly muley was not exactly tame, but he was accustomed to the ruckus of aviary patrons passing by. We asked Steve if we might borrow the handsome animal for a few days.

 We built a sturdy crate with a sliding door for the bed of the truck. Doug drove to the aviary the next day to load the buck. I stayed on set to do a scene with our wolf, Nero. When Doug arrived back on set that afternoon, there was a gash on the side of his head, and his shirt was ripped to reveal a long, deep-purple bruise on his rib cage. From the crate, peered the wide, gentle eyes of a doe. On-the-job animal trainer lesson number 14: never, truly never, mess around with a male ungulate while he is rubbing the velvet off his antlers and eating it. The velvet has been used in Asia for centuries as an aphrodisiac. The big muley had just finished his homegrown treat. I'm not sure what he wanted to do to Doug. Let's just say it wasn't pretty. One look at Doug inside his pen, and the buck turned into a Spanish fighting bull. Sadly, Doug's matador skills were sorely lacking. With Doug flat on the ground, Steve distracted the frenzied animal while Doug made his escape. Outside the pen, while checking Doug for broken ribs, Steve offered, "Maybe you should use the doe."

 As we moved through the weeks, we did fairly well as first-time professional animal trainers. Looking back now, I shudder to think how green we were. Our wild kids were tamed, true, but their training was basically Pavlovian. They would come to the sound of a bell or whistle or buzzer. The buzzer was the most versatile because we could hide the wire from button to buzzer and put the buzzer wherever the animal needed to go: in a tree, behind a rock, under a log. It worked alright, but it drove the sound department nuts.

 Some weeks into the show, Doug had driven down the mountain for supplies while I stayed with the animals. I was lying low in the camper shell with morning sickness, nibbling soda crackers and sipping raspberry leaf tea. Suddenly, I heard the rumble of two Harleys in the meadow. What the hell! I was supposed to be the security guard. I hopped out of the camper barefoot and disheveled in a nightshirt, and accosted the riders in their black leathers and even blacker shiny helmets. "I'm sorry," I said, "This is a closed set and private property; you will have to leave!" A helmet came off to reveal an extraordinarily handsome face. I had just kicked Robert Redford off his own mountain. He was really nice about it.

One animal we did have trained to a mark was Mizzer, the raccoon. I had achieved a new personal best in my emerging career as an animal trainer. I had worked for days on a master shot that called for Mizzer to climb through a window with a bullet in his hand (Yes, they do have hands), go to the fireplace, put the bullet down on an exact mark, and then exit through the window, all in one go. I was feeling confident and ready for my brilliant training moment. I had rehearsed it over and over with Mizzer. When the shot was up, I stuffed my pockets with Cheetos, his favorite treat, and whistled for him. He would not come down out of his aspen tree. The little varmint just looked down at me, kind of smiling.

That aspen tree was too tall and skinny to climb, or I would've grabbed him by his neck. It was the first time, but far from the last time, that I had that utterly helpless, embarrassed, sinking feeling on set. The whole cast and crew are waiting for you, looking at you, and your animal doesn't give a shit, and there is nothing you can do. Nothing. Except beg. The shot had to be pushed for two days until Mizzer got hungry enough to come down from his lofty perch. When I got out the little packs of vanilla pudding, our shot went beautifully. Nonetheless, I chopped down some aspen branches and fashioned them into an enclosure. Mizzer went to "the pen" for the rest of the shoot.

~~~~~~~~~~~~~~~~~~~~~~

I had raised the two tiny mule deer fawns on goat milk in Coke bottles with lamb nipples. They would come running to me whenever I called "bamp-bamp." They would follow me everywhere, and if I sat down, they would suck on my earlobes while I held skunks or whatever other baby animals needed to be on my lap at the moment.

"You know your baby can feel that," said a gentle voice behind me. I looked over my shoulder to see Burl Ives' wife, Dorothy, smiling sweetly at me. How on earth did she know I was pregnant? I hadn't mentioned it to anyone and was only eight weeks along. The lovely, ethereal woman became one of my first spiritual teachers. I could not dispute her account of past lives. She showed me an 1871 picture of Albert Pike, the Grand Commander of Free Masonry. It was the spitting image of Burl. I wondered if he'd had the same cotton candy voice. We visited for hours and hours between scenes. At the end of the show, she took off her gold bracelet and put it on my wrist. "This is to remind you of the circle of light that you must put around you and your baby. Never let anything that is dark or ugly inside of your circle."

I was never to see her again, but we wrote to each other for years, and I have the bracelet and the thought of the "circle of light" with me to this day.

Our last scene called for the kindly recluse to be writing at his small desk, with four or five baby skunks scampering around his journal. I was positioned under the table, pressed against Burl's grandfatherly legs. Every time a skunk would tumble off the table, I would catch it and put it back on his lap for the little stinker to crawl back up on the table. One little guy got tired and decided to curl up and take a nap on Burl's ample belly. We both giggled as the camera zoomed in for the super-sweet final shot of the movie.

It was the end of the show. Everything had basically gone very well. The words, "Thanks for a great job," meant as much as the paycheck — almost. We had beaten the catch-22; we now had a film credit for a major motion picture with major movie stars.

Leap

I have always loved the old fortune cookie adage, "The journey of 1,000 miles begins with one step." We had stumbled through a couple of those miles on the path that loomed before us: a mountaintop, a forest, the quest, the dream, and the leap.

Another movie was before us, although it was not so major. Over the east hills of Heber Valley, about 1,000 feet higher in altitude, the Kamas Valley rests quietly at the base of the Uinta Range. There lived one of the most irascible and singular men we would ever meet. His name was Dick Robinson, a Canadian, then in his 50s. His service in the Royal Canadian Air Force had earned him a metal plate where a piece of his skull should have been. It didn't seem to slow him down much. For years he had traveled about as a one-man carnival in a panel truck painted with colorful 1890s-era circus graphics proclaiming, "Ranger Rob and Willie the Wonder Bear." It was about as close as you could get to a reincarnation of James Capen Adams, the original Grizzly Adams of 1850s California fame. Somehow, Dick had landed in the Kamas Valley. He had attached himself to an early independent production company called Sunn Classic Pictures. Together, they had produced a film called *Brother of the Wind*, a story about an old man and his pack of wolves. We thought it was a fine independent film with some extraordinary theme music. It had been shot on a hand-wound 16mm Bolex camera. Doug and I had viewed the film in Los Angeles and had wanted to meet Dick ever since we moved to Heber City. I'm sure he saw us as wannabes, with our ragtag band of varmints, but we thought he was pretty cool.

In the film *Jeremiah Johnson*, it had been Dick's bear, Willie, that had chased Will Geer into the cabin and Robert Redford up a tree. The latter adventure had not been in the script. It was now a local legend that the scene was delayed because Willie, who had seldom been out of his cage, was having a blast chasing a ham tied to a rope. After numerous takes, Willie got bored and disappeared into the hills for three days. It was a different time back in the '70s; there weren't many rules about having your pet grizzly running loose in the wild. Dick hunted Willie down and lured him back into the "Wonder Bear Van" with bags of unwrapped Tootsie Rolls.

In any event, Dick was now temporarily on a roll writing and starring in his own independent films. The current project was a film called *Claws*. One scene called for a young man to be attacked by a grizzly bear. Guess who was the only person to audition for the part?

It wasn't really a matter of all balls and no brains. We had decided we needed some kind of killer, attention-getting photo for the cover of the brochure we were putting together for our new business, Wasatch Wildlife. For the right to use the photo, plus some transport cages and $300, Doug would wrestle Willie the Wonder Bear. Dick's bear wrestling advice to Doug

Wasatch Wildlife's first attempt at a brochure.

was, "Put a ham sandwich in your back pocket and then pull the hair on his belly," and, "Don't worry, he doesn't have any teeth." I climbed onto the roof of our truck to get a good vantage point for our cover photo. I could see Willie's teeth, all right. My husband might damn well die before my eyes. I can't remember how I stopped shaking long enough to snap the photo. It was rather blurry.

At the same time, Dick's production company was making a super-low-budget film called *Mountain Charlie*. It was the story of a girl from the East who heads into the Wild West in search of her father's killer. The film crew consisted of three people: camera, sound, and one all-purpose grip/gaffer/construction/prop man. Dick showed up to direct if and when the mood struck him. The laid-back set was great fun. No one was over 30, and we just made stuff up as the day went along, like kids with a camera in their own backyard. The location was a log cabin in the mountains. The creative freedom gave us a chance to sharpen our skills as animal trainers.

We trained our wolves to wear rubber leg traps and turned the raccoons loose on sacks of flour and jugs of maple syrup in the kitchen. We dropped skunks down the chimney to land in a bed of sawdust. The skunks chased the bad guys out of the cabin. As a bonus, I played the bar gal with a heart of gold. For a costume, I was handed a yard of red satin, an ostrich feather, and some safety pins to fasten the slippery fabric over my six-months-pregnant body. My boobs looked great, though.

We spent the last of our *Baker's Hawk* money piecing together our brochure, and there on the front cover was a picture of Doug wrestling a grizzly bear. We hand-addressed over 250 brochures to every production company listed in what was then the bible of the industry, the Studio Directory Guide. We wrote "please file for reference" on the back of each envelope. I suspect now that each and every one of our brochures ended up in a trash bin. We did know this: if we were ever going to make a living at our dream, we would need a bear … a big one.

Earlier that year, the Animal and Plant Health Inspection Service had paid us a visit to inform us that, if we were going to use our animals in films, we would need a USDA exhibitor's license. The rules were pretty basic back then: secure, sheltered enclosures kept very

Our dog Jake, baby Bart the Bear, and me the day before Sausha's birth.

clean, good feed, and proper vet care. We were found in compliance, and with our USDA license in hand, we started calling all the zoos listed on the International Species Information System report that listed brown bear cubs in their inventory for sale or transfer.

Doug's parents were horrified. "You can't do this," they said, "What are you thinking? You're going to have a baby. Get a real job!" Even Doug's college buddies said, "You can't do this, you Dumb Shit! Nobody just gets grizzly bears and makes them into movie stars. You can't do this!" That's all it took.

The Baltimore Zoo had two newborn male Kodiak cubs in the nursery. They were the result of an unplanned pregnancy. The zoo only had one bear enclosure and could not separate the male bear from the cubs. It wasn't safe for the cubs. There seemed to be no other zoo in the country at the time that had a need or a place for two little *Ursus arctos middendorffi*. The gods were with us. We sent a check for $50 and were informed that the cubs would arrive at 5 a.m. Tuesday at the Salt Lake City airport.

Again, it was a different time.

I was eight and a half months pregnant with undiagnosed pre-eclampsia. I looked like an orange as we drove up and over Parleys

Summit at 3 a.m. in a raging blizzard. A large dog crate was lifted over the counter at the air cargo desk. Inside were two silky brown lumps that looked like little deflated footballs with claws. We had brought a thermos bottle of formula and raced over to a friend's house in the city to feed them. Baby bears smell delicious, like pumpkin and butternut squash. To this day, I cannot carve a pumpkin or cut into a butternut squash without seeing baby grizzlies in my mind. The first time I picked up Bart, I held him like an infant, his head on my shoulder, front legs spread out on my chest, heart to heart. I had one hand on his back, the other cuddled tightly under his little butt. His right eye was still partially sealed shut; he had little pink feet that would fit inside the palm of my hand. I was to spend the next two decades loving that bear.

The cubs had been born in mid-January. It was now the end of February. They were six weeks old and weighed five pounds. At birth, they had weighed a pound and a half. This is one of nature's outstanding exercises in sound logic if you ask me. The cubs spend their first three months of life tight in the den with their mother. They are small and helpless. If they were born tearing around like little race cars, throwing fits, screaming, and chewing their mother's ears off, they might not live to get out of the den. I rather think it's this same logic that makes our huge-eyed human newborns so helplessly adorable. If our infants were born acting like two-year-olds, most couples would stop at one child. In that same wisdom, bear cubs don't even walk for the first two months of their lives.

We named the cubs Bart and Zack. They were to be raised in our kitchen until late spring. We spread the floor with blankets from the thrift store and had stacks of newspapers to be shredded as litter in their crates. Slowly, we separated them, intending that they would look to us, instead of each other, for warmth and comfort. We fed them every four hours. The sink was always full of soapsuds and baby bottles. A mother bear's milk is thirty percent fat, so our refrigerator was loaded with cartons of heavy cream and chicken necks waiting to be boiled down into a fatty broth. The cubs changed from footballs to bowling balls with short, thick legs and claws.

We held them closely as we fed them. I often wondered if my full-term human baby could feel the weight of the bear spirit covering her, separated by only a half inch of skin and womb. I could see the cubs responding to the sharp thumps and kicks under their bellies. During one late-night feeding, I didn't feel quite right. It was time to get the baby out from under the bears.

For many, the 1970s was the time of natural everything, organic to the core ... natural childbirth, breastfeeding, homemade yogurt, and organic carrot soup from your own garden. As we left for the hospital, I gathered the "focal point" pictures I had selected during our Lamaze classes. On the sea-foam green wall beside the delivery bed, I taped my photos of mountain meadows, clouds, and sunsets, a nest of mallard eggs, and my favorite Rocky Mountain wildflowers. Sausha was born at 9 a.m. on a snowy March morning — all six pounds of her. She was tiny, pink, and fragile. It seemed to make perfect sense that her middle name should be Fairyslipper, after the tiny, pink, fragile Rocky Mountain wild orchid. We left the Heber City hospital at 11 a.m. because we had no insurance, and besides, it was time to feed the bear cubs. The first thing we did when we got home was to prop up our newborn babe on the sofa and arrange two Kodiak cubs on either side of her for her birth announcement. Each weighed 6 pounds ... for about two days.

Doug with a six-pound baby Bart the Bear.

By September, the bear cubs outweighed Sausha by 100 pounds. The bears grew like images in time-lapse photography. However, reasoning that bears in the wild were still in the den (otherwise known as our kitchen), we stuck with the four-hour feeding schedule. That made for some sleepless nights. At 2 a.m. and 6 a.m., I had the newborn on the breast and the cubs on their bottles. Luckily, I never got them mixed up. If I had, it would have only happened once.

Any parent knows that the sound of a wailing infant cannot be tuned out. Sensitivity to that volume and pitch is hardwired into our brains. It cannot be ignored. It demands attention. My baby girl had a loud, healthy cry, but she could not hold a candle to the sound of the Kodiak cubs. Baby bears scream. They may be the world's loudest demand feeders. The sound is that of an injured pig, the bray of a Jenny mule, and the screech of a chainsaw, all put together by the "Master Sound Mixer." It must electrify every nerve ending on the mother bear's body. Her cubs will bowl her over and demand her nipples, then putter in delight. She likes it that way. That is what it will take for them to survive outside the den. All I can say is, pray

Sausha, at a few hours old, on the couch with Bart and Zack.

that you never come between that scream and a mother grizzly in the wild.

Every time a child is born, a mother is born. And every woman knows the moment the mother grizzly inside her is born ... "I will lay down my life for this tiny bit of flesh that has come through the blood and pain of my body. If you hurt her, I will kill you." Don't mess around with mother grizzlies.

The only time that Bart ever bit me was at a late-night feeding. I was probably dozing off and didn't get the nipple quite right in his mouth. In a flash, my hand was hit by a lightning-bolt. I was sure some of my metacarpals were broken. Bart only weighed about 20 pounds. Instinctively I flipped the baby bottle and knocked him sharply between the ears. Mother grizzlies don't allow their cubs to bite them. Bart chuffed and lowered his head, then looked up at me, softly.

In that moment we came to an understanding, that grizzly and me. I remember thinking, "Oh, dear God, what am I doing?" Little did I know what a life he would make for me.

Me, Doug, newborn Sausha, and baby Bart the Bear — when everything changed.

How to Train Your Grizzly

It was spring, and the days were generously lengthening as the summer solstice approached. Doug spent every daylight hour with the little Kodiaks. The task at hand was teaching them manners. Fortunately, bear cubs are programmed to accept discipline from their mothers. Our rules were pretty simple:

No, you cannot attack me for this peach in my hand.

No, neither may you scream and roar at me.

You, wild, primal, bear, will sit nicely and wait until I, the human, decide to give you this bottle of milk, when I am damn good and ready.

A bit easier said than done.

Extraordinary patience?

No, there never was, nor ever will be, a patient bone in Doug's body. Persistence, determination, endurance, and obsessive-compulsive will power? Yes.

A sheer will and a rage that matches that of a Grizzly. A unique power that borders on madness.

To become the world's greatest bear trainer, this madness must prevail.

I never could have done this part of the process. All I could do was gently imitate Doug's actions. But that's okay. There was a balance for the cubs, a formidable male force who they truly believed could kill them and eat their liver … and a Mother Grizzly they knew would never let that happen.

We Move to the Banks of Daniels Creek

The dormer-roofed 1919 farmhouse sat on a two-acre remnant quilt block that had been part of an 1876 quarter-section homestead. About 30 feet west of our side door, the original Swedish homestead cabin still sat square and firm on its river-rock foundation. Built without a single nail, its dovetailed logs had squeezed tighter and tighter together over a century. I imagined the surprise on a spectral Swedish face peering out from the tiny window in the loft of the cabin as the farmyard filled with two Kodiak bears, two cougars, five wolves, two bobcats, three foxes, five skunks, two raccoons, a buck and a doe, a hawk, an owl, and a badger. The actual shock and surprise were on the real-life faces of the neighbors, who looked like they were the ones seeing apparitions. Those wide-eyed neighbors would prove to be the most loyal of friends in a few short years.

We staked out an area for the smaller pens and enclosures along the creek bottoms. The shade and the stream were perfect, but it was September, and we only had about six weeks before the dark and cold. The Kodiak cages were a priority. My brother Mojo was a concrete contractor, and Doug could weld. We sold everything we had that was worth anything and bought 6-gauge corn cribbing, steel pipe, angle iron, and stacks of plywood and set to work. I put Sausha in a carrier and took care of feeding, cleaning, and nurturing all of us. Doug was building something somewhere from dawn to dusk. By the first snow, the bears were in their fortresses, 15 feet from our back door. We could talk to them from the kitchen table through a hedge of lilac branches.

I have heard it said that 33 is the age of genius. I'm quite sure I never got that chip, but I do know that I must have had some kind of nuclear energy. What Doug had was his obsession. Be it compulsive, determined, demented, or destined — it was magnificent.

As far as I know, there are no books written on the raising and training of Kodiaks. We taught ourselves to get inside their heads — and our own. We spent endless hours turning our backs and walking away from the bears when the yearling cubs screamed for the buckets of food in our hands. It took a while for them to understand that lesson in their bear brains: "Every time I roar at the bucket and the human, they go away. Goddammit, that makes me want to scream! Okay, okay, if I hold my rage for a second or two the bucket of food will be dumped at my feet."

We repeated the process over and over, walking toward them slowly and deliberately. Finally, prolonged silence! We dumped the food and said, "Good boy!" It only took about 100 times.

Now it was time to train the bears to walk on a lead. It's the same process as halter-breaking a colt; when the young horse bucks and sets back, you snap the lead rope, and the rope pops the tender muzzle. The animal then believes you are physically and mentally stronger, and you get to be the boss. The approach is not so different with a grizzly. We set a path from point A to point B and sledgehammered truck axles with custom-welded, three-quarter-inch steel swivel hooks deep into the ground, about 15 feet apart. Then, we double-wrapped a stout chain around the bear's neck and asked him to walk nicely beside us. When he bolted like a rabbit, we quickly wrapped the chain around a truck axle. As he hit the end of the chain and dumped on his head, we looked strong and pretended we had done it, saying, "Easy!" It only took about 100 times.

Doug decided to ride Bart and Zack bareback. The bears were about four feet high at the withers, and Doug's toes could almost touch the ground. I would get their attention and call them with a bucket of cookies. Doug would roll onto their backs and hold on to their humps with a stiff-armed grip. It wasn't so easy, as their skin rolled on their bodies like a fur coat lined with satin. The bears absolutely loved it. It only took about 100 times.

At the heart of everything were the relationships, the growing friendship, companionship, trust, and just plain love between the two species. Oh, there were some knock-down, drag-out moments that sent the neighbors running to their fences to see what the hell was going on. And there were times when I would think it was way too quiet, grab Sausha in my arms, and go out to find the three of them sleeping together like a pile of puppies.

~~~~~~~~~~~~~~~~~~~~

Grizzly Adams

The winter of 1977 offered us a big break with Bart's first national exposure. The NBC series *Grizzly Adams* was one of the most popular shows on television. The series was filmed in the Kamas Valley, a mere 26 miles east of us. To be clear, the bear in the series was named Bozo and belonged to a man named Lloyd Beebe, whose business, Olympic Game Farm, thrived in Sequim, Washington. Mr. Beebe was known for his work in early Disney true-life adventure movies. He had an impressive range of North American animals, from his giant Kodiak, Tag, and Bozo, the "Grizzly Adams' Bear," to cougars, wolves, black bears, every animal we had, and a lot more. He was also a very kind and decent man. Frankly, we were in awe of him.

Our good fortune came when NBC ordered a Grizzly Adams' Christmas special, but the Beebe animals were home in Washington for a winter break. A part of that Christmas special, "Once Upon a Starry Night," called for Grizzly Adams, played by Dan Haggerty, to be taking a Christmas hike through the mountains on a sparkling, sunlit day, all the while catching glimpses of wildlife in a winter wonderland.

We had known most of the series' production crew since we had

Bart the Bear at one year old with Doug, me, and Clint.

played together on our Dick Robinson movies. The producer knew of our fledgling efforts as Wasatch Wildlife. Our business card read: "Tame, Trained Animals for the Film and Television Industry at Fair and Reasonable Prices." We agreed to a deal to provide all our animals for $5,000. I remember thinking, "I can stretch this money for a year if I have to."

The director wrote the scenes around our cast of critters. Dragging cages and creatures through three feet of fresh Utah powder was butt-busting, but we pulled off some worthy shots:

A pack of wolves howling on a snowy ridgeline — their silhouettes against a fire-rimmed, salmon-pink sunrise, and bassoon tones suspended above their arched heads in frozen silver clouds.

Deer bounding down the mountainside like Olympic skiers on a slalom run.

Billy the Badger tunneling through the drifts like a plumber's snake, his little black and white face popping up here and there with a snow hat perched on top of his head.

The fox and coyotes jumping four-footed on "mice," which were, of course, our ubiquitous buzzers buried in the snow.

Our owl, Merlin, his unblinking, neon-yellow eyes staring out from a frosted blue spruce — so magical that one would never suspect he was a rescue bird with a missing wing tip.

Grizzly Adams looked lovingly on all of these scenes.

Then, it was time for the bear scene. Yep, we were finally in the "Bear League." The director had an idea — "How about Bart and Zack chase a raccoon up an aspen tree?"

"Umm ... Oh, sure, we can do that."

Oh, shit, but we really wanted to be invited back to be in another part of the series. Our plan was to let Bart and Zack play together around the tree. We planted a buzzer in the top of the aspen with jellybeans and let Mizzer out of his crate. Sure enough, the raccoon bolted out of his crate and bee-lined it for the jellybeans and his buzzer, jumping over the bears in his way. The shocked Kodiaks whirled in place, then pursued the masked varmint like army tanks. The game was on. Looking good until Bart got to the aspen, stood on his hind legs, and started to whiplash the tree back and forth like a huge fly rod.

Bart the Bear and our raccoon Mizzer on the Grizzly Adams' Christmas special.

One should remember to never, ever piss off a raccoon while it's eating jellybeans.

Mizzer launched out of the tree like a flying squirrel and made a four-point landing on Bart's head, right between his ears. In terror, Zack ran back to the safety of his trailer. Bart spun like a rodeo bull, trying to dislodge the crazed raccoon, who had a death grip on his head and was sinking his little fangs into Bart's furry ears and forehead. Frantically, we threw jellybeans into Mizzer's crate and buzzed him from his eagle-talon hold on Bart's head. The camera cut away to Dan Haggerty, who was laughing so hard he couldn't stand up in the snow.

We added Grizzly Adams "Once Upon a Starry Night" to our credit list and made it through the winter with firewood and food for everybody.

"Hey, Man, Are You Sure You Know What You're Doing?"

There truly could not have been a better time for us to launch our movie animal business. The mid-'70s and into the '80s was the era of wilderness adventure films fashioned from the buckskin of the Grizzly Adams series. The Wilderness Family Adventures, Across the Great Divide, The Deer Slayer, and the like were all shot on location in Utah. We were the extra animal trainers on set and oftentimes overheard the Los Angeles trainers refer to us as "Little Local Union 299." The major animal players and trainers were the big companies from Los Angeles; their studio union was 399. We took the leftover bit parts and pieces and were glad to have them. If we didn't have the animal the script called for, we would find it somehow, somewhere. We sourced beavers from fur farms. It was humbling and wearing, standing in icy mountain streams holding onto the big rodents by their fat, slick tails (that's the only way they couldn't bite you with their huge choppers), waiting for the cue to release them downstream into frame, but it was paying work.

One of our bit parts was for Sunn Classic Pictures' rendition of James Fennimore Cooper's classic, *The Deer Slayer*, starring Steve Forrest. One scene was thus: young lovers walk through a mountain meadow full of wildflowers. The boy reaches down to pick a blossom for his sweetheart when a little covey of partridges flutters up and startles them into giggles and kisses. We bought four pairs of Hungarian partridges from a local game bird farm. We also purchased a bird releaser, a box-like contraption with a spring mechanism in the bottom that pops the top open and flings the birds up when a trigger wire is pulled. We were sure it would be easy.

The day we picked up the partridges, the owner of the bird farm told Doug of a little trick to quiet the birds a bit before we placed them in the releaser. "Here's what you do," he explained, "Hold the little guys upside down and gently spin their heads in a circle. This mesmerizes the birds, and they go to sleep

One of my great teachers, our wolf Peach.

for a minute or two." Great idea! The next day before the shot, I hid the releaser in the tall meadow flowers. Doug proceeded to get the birds "relaxed." The assistant director looked on and said, "Hey man, are you sure you know what you're doing?" "Oh, hell yeah! I've done this hundreds of times," replied Doug.

The camera was rolling; the sweet couple strolled through the meadow, and the boy reached down to pick the flowers ... Okay, I hit the release trigger. The birds popped up in the air, alright, breast up, heads hanging down backwards. Dead — like those cartoon birds with Xs for eyes. The couple looked up in wonder as the birds rose. Their heads dropped in unison as the partridges fell back to the ground.

We were mortified. The director yelled, "Print it! Print it!! I've got to see this again!"

Of course, the real animal trainers from Los Angeles were all on set watching. We were humiliated, but not for the last time.

That same summer, we received one of our first calls for a bear in another wilderness feature film, *Frontier Fremont,* the story of John C. Fremont's early mapping of the West. The scene was to be a cutaway of a grizzly bear deep in the forest. Our USDA Animal and Plant Health Inspection Service regulations and Utah Division of Wildlife Resources license call for all "dangerous predators" to be contained while out of their permanent enclosures and trailers. These are the same regulations that require netting around a big cat act in the circus. In film work, especially before the days of computer-generated images, the animal had to appear to be free in the wild. The answer is a portable safety fence of electrified, 24-gauge steel wire. The zap comes from a battery. The system has been used on cattle ranches for years — the same fencing that country boys dare each other to pee on. I've been zapped by the wire countless times. While it gets one's attention, it is not nearly as bad as the shock from fishing a piece of bread out of a toaster with a fork.

We had been training the cubs to stay behind their wire. We thought we were ready to do a shot of a bear free in a dense forest. We set up the electric perimeter fence and pulled the trailer into place. We had decided to use Zack, as he was bigger and more impressive than Bart.

It was time for the bear scene. We opened the trailer door; Zack took one look at the dark forest and wanted no part of it. He would not budge from the safety of his trailer, his "den." One does not force a Kodiak.

No problem, we had a backup bear. We opened Bart's trailer door, and he bolted out of the trailer and ran right through the wire like it wasn't there, disappearing into the forest — YIPPEE!!! Doug was wearing a red and white western shirt that day. All anyone, including the camera, could see or hear was a red-and-white blur yelling, "Bart! Bart! You little shithead, come back here!" Bart never even turned his head to look back at Doug. The very happy, dashing, smashing, wild, two-year-old Kodiak charged through the forest, taking out small trees like a bulldozer. The camera got glimpses of a bear deep in the forest — he just happened to be running. To this day, it makes me laugh when I think about it, but believe me, it wasn't so damn funny to Doug at the time. Humiliation notwithstanding, we must have been doing something right because we received a call that elated us.

A TV miniseries based on James Michener's *Centennial* was in full production on the South Platte River near the small town of Orchard, Colorado, 40 miles northeast of Denver. The epic series spanned the story of Colorado from the mid-1700s to the late-1970s. A scene with Richard Chamberlain and Robert Blake, portraying French voyageurs of the fur-trading era, called for wolves. I still don't know how the producers found out about us, but they asked us to be on location with a pack of five wolves in three days. Oh my gosh, Wasatch Wildlife would work on a major series with major stars! It was easy enough to get my brother to take care of Bart and the other animal kids, and my mother would watch over Sausha. But I had to take along three one-week-old coyote pups that needed to be bottle-fed every four hours. We put the tiny coyotes in a crate, loaded up the wolves, and hurried east on I-40 to the South Platte River.

When we arrived, the production was a day behind. We were to stand by on call. We spent the day handing out our brochures to anyone who would take them (A bit embarrassing to think about now). The director, Virgil Vogel, kept glancing over at Doug, whose big, audacious beard was rather eye-catching. When he headed over to us, I wondered if we were going to be asked to leave the set. "You look like a mountain man," he said to Doug and then hurried away for a waiting shot. Over the years, we were to work with Mr. Vogel on other films calling for wolves and bears. He would always find a small part or a few lines for Doug. He thought Doug should have been an actor. The only problem was the mountain man guy had absolutely no acting talent. None whatsoever. Best stick to bear training.

Production put us up for the night at the 4-star hotel where the rest of the crew was staying. We were able to leave the wolf trailer on set with security. The hotel had a strict no-pet policy, so I smuggled the coyote pups and their baby bottles in my backpack up to our room, where we hid them in a dresser drawer for the night. Thank goodness they were too young to set off righteous coyote yelps.

The next morning, our wolf shot was up first. The scene called for the voyageurs to land their raft on the near bank of the river, look up, and suddenly see a pack of wolves waiting for them. We had been working diligently at training our wolves to come to a mark for the camera. They were trying, but they were as new to the business as we were. They were in place, and the cameras were rolling, but the scary sight of two fully costumed voyageurs coming at them with oars was not worth staying on their marks for chicken necks. Another humiliation.

Me helping Richard Chamberlain feed a coyote pup on the set of *Centennial*.

I grasped at a thought. Wolves cannot resist any young canine with puppy breath — the smell of coffee and honey. They *must* — they have to — take care of pups. It is deeply and innately programmed in them. I ran to the truck, stashed the coyote pups in my coat pockets, and dashed back to set. We called the wolves to their marks. They could not resist the reward of being able to nuzzle and lick the tiny coyotes. They held their marks. We got the shot.

Immediately afterward, Richard Chamberlain walked up to us, "Please, may I hold them?" he asked. He snuggled the tiny cubs on his lap and stroked them softly, saying, "Oh, my sweet little pups." We were delighted that America's heartthrob would hold up production time to cuddle and bottle-feed our coyote pups. We headed back to Utah with a gleeful heart and another major credit for our growing resume.

The Decision

We spent the remainder of the summer trying to find enough hours in a day for the intense training of both Kodiaks. I took care of the other animals with Sausha either on my back or in a Clorox-scrubbed 4x6 cage with a blanket, toys, and animal crackers. The sight of a toddler in a cage provoked raised eyebrows and daunting looks from passersby, but thankfully, they were not upset enough to call Family Social Services. The neighbors were used to seeing the two-year-old in the cage, like a playpen with a top, and knew she was safe, clean, and happy within sight of her mother. The animals were accustomed to the little, two-legged cub and looked for her; if she was inside the house napping, they noticed her absence.

We continued Bart and Zack's daily training. By now, the bears were familiar sights throughout the valley. Our objective was to get them accustomed to stressful situations so that the generators, wind machines, camera cranes, and such on movie sets would not be big, scary surprises. I don't like 18-wheelers roaring past me at 80 miles per hour; I can't think grizzly bears like it either. So, one step in our stress training was to acclimate the bears to the sight and sound of tractor-trailers. Highway 40 is also Heber City's Main Street, and though it was not as busy back then, we had our share of semis ripping through town. We parked the bear trailer on Main Street at Heber City's only stoplight. Doug would stand beside the trailer with a bag of marshmallows, and each time a big rig would rumble by and the bears faced it, he would pop in a fluffy treat. He did that for hours.

Another good stress-training site was the local sawmill, with the ear-splitting screech of the buzz saw. It was a stressful place for the bears, and also for Doug and me. It reminded Doug that he might have to go back to work there if we didn't make a go of our business. I was unnerved by the place. It sounded to me like the trees were screaming as they were being dismembered. We also spent hours at helicopter pads, parades, firework displays, skeet ranges, and feed mills.

With each stress-training day, it became ever more evident that Zack was not cut from the same cloth as Bart. Although Zack was much bigger than Bart and very gentle, the critical difference was that Zack saw life as a serious drama, and Bart saw it as a situational comedy. There was not only the question of whether Zack would ever be able to handle a movie set, but whether it would it be psychological torture to ask him to try.

There was another consideration: chicken, even freezer-burned and outdated, now cost 30 cents a pound, and we were feeding them 120 pounds a day. Zack continued to do no better. It became obvious that he was stressed by strange and noisy places. He was only happy at home in his familiar den, or in the backyard with Doug and me. On the other hand, Bart could hardly wait for his next action adventure.

For all these reasons — plus the fact that there was another human baby on the way — we made a difficult decision.

The American Association of Zoos and Aquariums had a list of zoos that were expanding and animals they might need. We began checking accredited USDA APHIS zoo listings to see if there was a place where Zack could just be at home. On the list was the Lincoln Children's Zoo in my hometown of Lincoln, Nebraska. A coincidence ... or was it?

In my childhood, I had walked through the 1950 zoo grounds in Memorial Park on my way home from school. The zoo's curator had known my grandparents well and was overjoyed to hear about

Doug with Bart the Bear and Zack at three months old.

Zack. The zoo would launch a fundraiser to build a two-acre, tree-lined habitat with a moat, a pool, and a den. We were to deliver Zack to Lincoln. They told us the exhibit would be ready by early November. That seemed a good time of year, as the weather would be cool, and we should arrive before the winter storms. We lined up friends and family to take care of Bart and the other animals, loaded grass hay, chicken, apples, and Zack in the trailer, put Sausha in a car seat in the pickup, and set off on the 1,000-mile trek from Heber City to Lincoln, Nebraska.

The blizzard hit us where Interstate 80 crosses the Medicine Bow River between Rawlings and Laramie, Wyoming, at a spot called Elk Mountain. It was about 6 p.m., and we knew we had to get off the highway. There was a ranch exit, number 72 onto Rattlesnake Road, that led to jeep trails in the Medicine Bow Mountains. Through the driving, hypnotic snow, we could just make out the yellow light of what looked like a trailer-sized store. As we pulled into the tiny parking lot, the interior light was switched off. Doug jumped out of the truck and pounded on the door. The light came back on, and an indifferent, middle-aged man let us in. No, there was no lodging any closer than Laramie, 50 miles east. No, it was not possible to put some blankets on the floor and spend the night. We bought a jar of chipped beef, some crackers, and a can of evaporated milk for

Sausha.

As we made our way back outside, the truck and trailer were barely visible, already covered with a foot of snow. Inside the truck, I held onto my tender two-year-old while Doug managed to find the chicken and apples for Zack. Interestingly, the bear was relaxed, sleeping calmly in his trailer; it was a familiar space, and he felt safe. As the snow blew and deepened, I remembered my great-grandfather's farm in Table Rock, Nebraska. There was a rope strung between the kitchen door and the barn, a stone's throw away. I was told the rope was there so one could find the way back to the house in a blizzard. I hadn't believed it — until now.

We took out the car seat and tried to comfort Sausha and keep her warm between us. We used the heater intermittently to try to save our quarter-tank of gasoline. During the long night, Doug, who was just about as good at handling stress as Zack, was raging and ready to turn around and go back to Utah. The wailing of my two-year-old and the fluttering of the baby in my belly led me to plead desperately that we continue to Lincoln. I knew in my heart that we needed to concentrate physically, emotionally, and financially on just one Kodiak. I knew my stamina had a limit, and that our dream demanded that it be limitless. The blizzard spent itself through the night, but the wind continued to howl like a tortured violin. I was terribly sick by the time we got to Lincoln, but my reasoning had prevailed.

We had asked the zoo's curator to close the exhibit and hold off the press for a couple of days while Zack settled into his new surroundings. He hung out in his commodious den at first, then ventured out to his playground, pool, and moat. We stayed by him until it became clear that he was not only relaxed but also felt content and safe. That was all good, but when it was time to walk away, we were both in tears and could not look back.

Knowingly, Zack chuffed out a cry. I thought that must be what it feels like to give up a baby for adoption. The empty trailer haunted us. We did not talk much on the way home. Had we given away a part of our dream? Doug was in a depression until spring.

The sound of a Lark on a summer morning

Liquid notes of foreboding laughter that slowly sputter out

like an old-time phonograph running out of power

Then the silence

The dark descending, twisting tornado knows nothing but itself

Do not try to stop the torrent or it will inhale and consume you

Best to let the blackness torment its own until it gasps for air

Never get too close to the event horizon or your own light will be

Sucked out

Let it be

There will come the Lark

Pushing Through

Jedediah Jacob Seus was late — almost two weeks overdue, to be exact. It proved to be a lifetime trait; he liked to sleep in. But enough is enough. Time to rise and shine, little dumpling boy! There were two wolf pups and a baby black bear in crates in the kitchen, and my basketball belly presented quite a problem when bending over.

The country doctor put me on an intravenous Pitocin drip to induce labor, then went about his calls. Jed literally popped into this world with only the nurse and Doug to receive the slippery forward pass. The doctor didn't show up for another three hours. Perhaps he was still ticked off at me for a little joke I had played on him the week before.

Doug and I had received a few calls on scripts that specifically required a black bear, so we decided we needed to add one to our cast of animal actors. Black bears — all bears — are born in the den in late winter; early spring is the only time to get a cub. We decided to go for it, despite the fact there would be a human baby too. After all, we had done it before.

Jack, the black bear cub, was now about six weeks old and weighed about six pounds. At nighttime bottle feedings, I held him wrapped in a blanket on top of my belly.

When a woman is 37 weeks pregnant and counting, doctor appointments are usually scheduled one week apart. I had a doctor's appointment the next morning. Hmm …

Sausha at three years old with Jack, our six-week-old black bear cub.

I gave Jack his morning feeding right before I left for the clinic. The cub was content and sleepy as I wrapped him in a baby blanket and put him in an infant carrier. The nurse who showed me into the examining room was delighted to conspire with me. I got on the exam table, concealing my still bulging belly with the swaddled baby bundle. The nurse scurried down the hall, calling for the doctor to come quickly, "Lynne Seus had her baby at home this morning!" The stoic doctor, who was also a Mormon bishop, entered the room. "Well, well, well, what do we have here?" Drawing on my residual acting skills, I replied, "Well, the labor was very quick and easy, and I think everything is okay; I just want you to check out the baby." I flipped back the blanket, and the infant-size bear cub let out a scream.

The doctor gasped and staggered back. The heads of the nurses and receptionists, hands over mouths, were totem-poled, peeking through the crack of the door. The good doctor recovered and said, "I'm going to get you for this."

Perhaps he missed the real delivery because he didn't want any more surprises. The story was retold in Heber City for years.

~~~~~~~~~~~~~~~~~~~~~~~

I can't remember ever being busier than I was that spring. Sleep didn't seem to be an option. Thankfully, Jed was a mellow and content infant, oblivious that Sausha glared at him as she shared space on my lap. She seemed to have no such resentment for the time and space I gave to Jack, the bear cub, and the wolf babies, Peach and Yukon. My little dethroned princess seemed to know that the new, two-legged cub was not going to end up outdoors with the others. Doug was ever outside caring for the animals and spending endless hours with Bart. I kept the windows open and the door ajar to hear what was going on. Many times, I whisked the human babies into their cribs and ran outside to referee. I kept a heavy broom by the back door.

That special spring held another gift for us. We were hired to do a film that would become an anthropological classic, *Windwalker*. The director, Kieth Merrill, would become a lifelong friend, as did Reed Smoot, the cinematographer. The project was set in the Rockies in the late 18th century. The characters were all Native American, and the dialogue was spoken authentically in Crow and Cheyenne. It is the tale of an old Cheyenne warrior who has more than one life-changing encounter with a grizzly bear. At the beginning of the story, the young Windwalker, played by James Remar, saves his 2-year-old son from a grizzly that is dragging the child from camp. The scars that the boy carries for life have great significance later in the story. The elder Windwalker was played by Trevor Howard, a British star who seemed an unlikely Native American but played the part well. Ultimately, he kills the bear in a dramatic scene that was pivotal in our professional journey.

Windwalker would be the first on-screen film credit for Doug Seus and Bart the Bear. Doug would play opposite Bart in body paint, a brain-tanned breechcloth, a waist-length black wig of human hair, and beaded moccasins. In prep, we added a new element of the wardrobe every day to get Bart used to it. Bart may have thought Doug was having an identity crisis, but he seemed to find it interesting.

Teaching Bart to accept, and even enjoy, being stabbed by a prop spear and knife was more of a challenge. It was 1980, and every frame of the 35 mm film was for real. We had no blue screens, split screens, computer-generated images, or bear suits to cheat with. We just did it. We started rehearsing the spear-stabbing scene by purchasing about one hundred eight-foot long, three-inch diameter balsa-wood rods. We would have Bart stand on his hind legs and then hold up a rod for him to snap like a matchstick with his foreleg. Bart thought it was great fun; in fact, it was one of his favorite games. (When we would take him to the mountains for a romp, he loved to snap young aspen trees in half just to hear them break and crack, like a kid popping air pillows in bubble wrap.) We progressed to pine rods with rubber spearheads. The prop knife was also made of rubber, and the spring-loaded blade would retract into the handle on the "stab." Bart loved it. It tickled.

Now, for dragging the two-year-old boy from camp. We asked the art department to make us four practice dummies for Bart to rip to shreds. After three or four deaths of the dummy canvas child, Bart decided all that sand inside was boring. Fetching a dummy to us in exchange for a peanut butter jelly sandwich was a lot more fun. We progressed to the life-like child, which had a flesh-colored body, a black wig, jointed arms, and legs with little fingers and toes. From a distance, the prop looked disturbingly real. It was even more disturbing to see Bart drag the thing around. For over a year after the shoot, that life-like dummy gave me a start every time I walked into the prop shed until I finally put it in a box.

The climactic scene of the film called for the bear to be abruptly awakened from his winter sleep when the snow above the den gives way, and Windwalker falls on him. A fight ensues, and the old Cheyenne stabs the bear to death with a knife. The scene was shot on a sound stage at the Osmond Studio in Provo. It was our first sound stage experience. Basically, it was just a big house, and Bart got to come inside and play. We prepped Bart in his new playhouse for two days. Doug, dressed as the old Cheyenne, would get inside the cave and roll around with him, poking him in the ribs with the rubber knife. The cave became Bart's personal fun-tunnel.

It came time for his big scene with the principal actor. Mr. Howard, in full makeup and costume, walked on the set with a production assistant on each arm to steady him. It seemed the famous English actor had imbibed a bit of British bravery in vodka-injected oranges. With raised eyebrows and sideways glances, the two young men gracefully guided the bleary Sir Trevor to his position in the cut-away cave.

We walked Bart onto the set. He had rehearsed in the cave and was excited at the prospect of the "spear game" and cookies. Perhaps it was the energy field and aura of a 1,000-pound, three-year-old Kodiak. Whatever it was, it seemed that "the brave maker" (as the Western artist Charles Russell called alcohol) instantly evaporated from Sir Trevor's mind, and the venerable actor was as clear as a mountain stream. Doug put Bart on his mark and knelt out of frame between the two. Bart stud-

Doug and Bart the Bear's first big movie stunt for *Windwalker*.

ied his co-star. Sir Trevor studied Bart. The chemistry between them was instantaneous.

So it happened that Bart had his first close-up two shot with a world-famous face. There would be more, many more.

Always we learned. Always Bart taught us. Ever the trust, love, and camaraderie between our two species deepened.

Whose Life?

Spring had been terrific. Now, summer and fall stretched before us. One easy day we were hanging out with our friend George Stapleford, who was a brilliant cameraman from our Dick Robinson and Grizzly Adams days. As we looked out on our compound full of predators, we kicked around an idea of pitching a project to National Geographic Films. For a small budget, Wasatch Rocky Mountain Wildlife would produce our own film called *The Predators*. To our astonishment, National Geographic bought the idea. From animal trainers to producers! We were elated. But in the course of our new success, Doug and I both would have wake-up calls — reality checks that would have us almost losing our lives, or at least major body parts. These were lessons we needed to learn.

Our script simply worked its way up the predator food chain, starting with a shrew eating a grub. A shrew, one of those whiskered, little, tawny hornets you *maybe* think you see darting over the forest floor while you're hiking. Should be easy to catch one, right? Wrong. We spent hours in the Uinta Mountains with butterfly nets and live-capture mousetraps. The elusive shrew — as hard to catch as a house fly.

Finally, we offered a BYU summer botany class $50 if they could bring us a common shrew. About a month later, we were well into the rest of the shoot when we received a call from the professor. The class had just captured a shrew, and they were rushing it up Provo Canyon.

The metabolism of a shrew is such that they must eat constantly throughout the day; they can starve in an hour or so. We made a frantic call to George, who dropped everything and dashed up and over Parleys Summit from Salt Lake City. Doug and I got the "set" ready, a large glass terrarium dressed with moss, little logs, wild plants, and grubs.

The BYU students rushed up the driveway just as George was setting up his camera. We gently released the tiny, spiky rodent into the terrarium. It zipped onto a mossy stick and dropped over dead. I mean, it just up and died right then and there, with the camera rolling and the students staring on. Stunned silence. Then, an idea.

We moved the set dressing from the terrarium to our pine tree in the front yard. We propped up the little, fuzzy body with hidden toothpicks, got a hair dryer, set it on low, and made his whiskers and little muzzle move so he looked alive, then put a grub in his mouth. It worked. Well enough, anyway. It was better than a computer-generated image, which didn't even exist at that time of hand-held 16mm Bolex cameras.

Moving along with the production — a rattlesnake eating a mouse was even better filmed in slow motion.

Next up was a red-tailed hawk preying on a Uinta "potgut." (For some reason, the origin of which is known only to some Utah pioneer, ground squirrels are locally known as potguts.) However, there didn't seem to be any potguts about in our valley. I believe they had succumbed years before to neighborhood target practice. So, again, we went to the Uinta Mountains and easily captured several potguts by pouring water down their burrows and then, fishing net in hand, waiting at the entrance for them to emerge. We hauled a crate of them home and showed our hawk, Wilma, what was in it. She cocked her head to get a better look. We set Wilma soaring over our back field, opened the door of the crate, and let her potgut lunch escape. She knew exactly what to do, but there was a slight problem. She took out just one of the bushy-tailed rodents we had released. For a couple of years, Daniels Creek residents were befuddled by their ravaged tomato plants. "Where did all the damn potguts come from?" Umm …

Billy the Badger was in heaven when we took him to a creek bottom riddled with vole tunnels. He had a blast and gained five pounds.

Our foxes, hunting for field mice, performed their incredibly graceful arching pounce onto the small rodents.

The raccoons went hand-fishing for minnows and crawdads. Yummy. Now mind you, we didn't write the script; it was written by the master scriptwriter — Mother Nature.

About 70 miles southwest of our valley, there is a soft, rolling stretch of sage flats with mysterious granite outcroppings — the broad and silent Sevier River Valley. It is comprised of Bureau of Land Management grazing allotments that can support maybe one cow per 10 acres. The valley is also full of jackrabbits. It was there that we decided to film our wolves hunting their natural snack. And it was there I received my reminder.

At that time, we had eight wolves. For the scene, we used two females, Tundra and Lady, and three males, Koda, Yukon, and Teton. Like all our animals, they had been bottle-raised before their eyes had opened. Lady was the alpha female; in fact, she was basically the alpha of the entire pack. Lady loved me as a cub loves its mother. She would roll on her back and whimper and pee in pure delight as I rubbed her tummy.

I was about three months out from giving birth, and my breasts were overflowing with milk and probably the last few molecules of colostrum. Between nighttime newborn feedings of all the babies and dealing with a three-year-old who was still not overjoyed about sharing attention with her baby brother, and Doug, who had postpartum depression for me, I'd had little time to run with our five wolves. I was ecstatic to return to work that day in such a remote setting, with wolves running free.

The day was beautiful — cool, with sun and elephant clouds. Our caravan of wolves, camera crew, and big, brawny friend, Larry, a welder by trade and an occasional extra hand, set off for the West Desert. The area was so remote there was not another car in sight as we set up the camera. I had let Koda, Teton, and Yukon out of the trailer, and they were already running circles around each other. I was eager to release Lady. Her tail was wagging like crazy as I opened the trailer door, and she greeted me as usual, her paws on my shoulders. Then she bared her fangs.

It must have been the scent of my breast milk. Her fire-yellow eyes dilated to black; she spit out a snarl and lunged for my face. I reflexively covered my face with my elbow and was knocked backward, flat on the ground. I could feel the sagebrush and rocks against my spine as she pinned me. I could hear hate in her throat.

Larry was right behind me and grabbed Lady by the nape of her neck and her hips and hurled her into the trailer. She charged back against the inner door of the trailer just as Larry slammed it shut. It took me a second to comprehend what had just happened. Quivering, I got my feet under me as she hit the door again. She wanted to, and would have, killed me. Why? Had the alpha female been usurped by another female giving birth before she did? Did she want my pups? To mother them, or to kill them? I would have to figure all that out later, as the camera was in place and the other wolves were finding rabbits.

Lady never changed her mind about me. Interestingly, she still loved Doug, George, even Larry, and just about everyone else, but I had betrayed the alpha female, and I was not to be forgiven.

Another day, another location, and the last shot for the ultimate food chain film: a grizzly bear running off a pack of wolves from their deer kill. It had not been a problem to find a fresh carcass for the scene; road-killed deer are, unfortunately, common in the state of Utah. We placed the carcass not far from a stand of cottonwoods and sagebrush. We pulled the wolf trailer to one side of the grassy field, and Bart's trailer to the other.

The wolves could not believe their luck when they discovered a venison buffet in the tall grass. I have asked Doug to put the rest of the story into his own words, for it was totally his and Bart's experience.

The Test

Our National Geographic film was an educational project about the behavior of North American predators. I had doubled everyone's rations in anticipation of the final scene to reduce the chances of injury, and was well confident that everything would go smoothly. As pups, the wolves had played with Bart in his cubhood, and all parties had enjoyed the mix — getting along beautifully. Wolves are born coded for teamwork, and group dynamics are determined early through games. Hierarchy, however, is not always set in stone. It changes frequently amongst youngsters and less often in seniors. Bears are solitary and pretty much bulletproof in encounters with other species.

We received permission from the Utah Division of Wildlife Resources to use a doe that had been hit on a highway, and the next day, an officer delivered the carcass to our compound. We knew of a meadow in the high country that was often graced with radiant sunsets. On the day of the shoot, enthusiasm and professional accord ran high among the camera crew. Our safety meeting started a nervous chatter among several team members, so I delayed the shoot for an hour to review the protocol and alleviate their fears.

We cabled the doe to the ground to ensure that equipment wouldn't need to be moved in case the carcass was dragged from the camera's focus. As they burst from their trailer, six male wolves hurdled over one another's backs in a frenzied dash for first meat. The two alphas, Yukon aside Teton, shot to the front. The four subordinates, Koda, Legend, Spirit, and Shadow, closed on them fast. All six hit the carcass at once; however, pack harmony was disrupted when the two leaders denied the others a share of the coveted heart, liver, and intestines. Teton overstepped his status by swiping the liver from Yukon, and the two alphas began snarling over the other prime parts. Teton's boldness tested the patience of his older brother, and Yukon pinned him to the ground, letting him know he was out of line. After Teton's correction, Yukon invited him to return as his sharing partner. The others, stuffed on deer hindquarters, grew listless.

From within his trailer, Bart studied the madness. Upon release, his withers were two feet from the dirt before, face first and at full speed, he plunged into all the living and dead flesh. Watching Bart tear huge chunks from a rear flank, the camera crew fell silent with fear. Realizing their plan had failed, the six Lobos reunited in teamwork side-by-side. Legend and Shadow advanced, full of juvenile brashness. Legend saw a hunk of meat drop from Bart's mouth and headed for it. Shadow moved to Bart's rear to assist Legend's efforts with harassment. Bart anticipated Shadow's move and, with a counterclockwise twist, Bart stopped him short. A vertical leap landed Shadow a safe distance away atop a clump of sagebrush. Koda, a precocious personality, found random scraps of flesh scattered afar. Realizing that injury loomed, the wolves surrendered.

We knew we had the shot needed. Lynne and Larry gathered five of the pack; I rounded up the sixth. After trailering the wolves, I started for the deer carcass. Reveling in his success, Bart lay rug-like 10 feet from the remains. I received only a few high-minded peeks as I approached him before also stopping 10 feet short of the remains on the opposite side. Even with his disguise of indifference, I recognized that the stakes were raised. Familiarity breeds complacency, and being hardheaded, I was "all in." Common sense, I believe I have, but patience has never been my forte. I needed to own that prey. I continued my approach, stopping three feet from the deer.

Bart bolted upright and planted himself atop the carcass, straddling its ribcage. A primal roar confirmed I was deep in shit. A storm began to rage in my gut. Bart was defiant, and rightfully so. Fueled by fury, I was determined to win at all costs. I came within reach of the trophy. Bart did not flinch; his eyes pinned mine, flashing with a haunting, unforgettable fire. I moved closer and bent forward to grab the deer. The bear exploded — molten-like, consumed by madness. His energy devoured everything around us, creating an impenetrable barrier of dominance, climbing, widening, and pulsating with the forbidding message, "DO NOT ENTER." But I was already there.

Bart the Bear claims victory over a deer carcass in *The Predators*.

Bart's head swung horizontally, and he stomped to back me off. A portentous beast, Bart blew viscous mists from his mouth. He searched my face, then jerked, ripped, and clawed at the cable. It snapped. Shoveling and piling the meat under his chest, he owned it. Bart's jaws popped and chomped, metamorphizing him into a bomb. Razored keen and edged like a piece of obsidian, I made a snap decision to seize the largest hunk of flesh, the disjointed piece that he had so feverishly defended, and claimed it mine. Bart's head dropped below his withers, touching sagebrush. Then, as one compressed mass of muscle, he squeezed every bit of emotion into his hind legs — a foreboding omen. I grabbed for a length of wood to defend myself. Mouth agape, Bart lunged for my face — two different species compelled to battle, adrenalines dark and intermixed, entangled in each other's wrath, clashing in primitive warfare. Adrenaline boiling in my blood made me feral — robbed me of my good judgment but saved my life. I swung the wood, which caught the crown of his head. Momentarily stunned, he remained a big, big bear. Bart gathered his wits and surprised me when he came again. I landed a forearm under his jaw. I was too far in not to complete the journey. Our eyes invaded each other's. Understanding who we were, Bart yielded.

A bear's feet tell the story. He transferred all weight onto his two front legs, his rear toes merely tapped the earth, indicating the threat has passed A grumble replaced what was once a roar and gave me a moment to breathe. I called for the pickup truck to haul away the deer's remains. As it passed, I threw the flank held under my arm into the truck bed. With the battle prize removed and figs as consolation, I returned Bart to his trailer.

Bart and I were born of one fire. From three months old, we had romped daily. After five years, our rapport was solid. I never anticipated a need for a more relevant education. The events of that day became my obsession — I needed to repair the damage I thought I may have caused with the encounter. Mending our relationship needed to be hands-on; it would be measured deep in fur.

I never questioned my decisions from the previous day, but the next steps had me worried. I felt our foundation had not been destroyed. Perhaps it was cracked, but plenty of concrete still existed to build on. Patching wounds would be high stakes, exceedingly so. If all went well, more profound bonds would form between us, carrying our friendship into unexplored territory. Procrastination makes me apprehensive. A fretful night set my decision in stone — the test would take place the following day.

The next morning, Bart returned to his shelter after enjoying hours of swimming. From outside his shelter, Lynne kept him occupied with fruits and allowed me unimpeded entry to his quarters, which was crucial. I pulled a 25-pound remnant of the deer out of our cooler. The cut of flesh I chose had a purpose; it was a remnant of the event, bloodied, bone-embedded, and tending a hint rancid. It was imperative Bart stay beside me until he fulfilled his hunger, and that any resentment from the previous day be put to rest. This could only be accomplished by fastening the meat to my body so he couldn't carry it away and eat alone. The gadget — a snap-link swivel — was my own invention. I *inserted a short 18-gauge wire through 12 inches of bone and flesh. Then, I looped 10 inches of clothesline around my wrist and bound it to the assembled parts — marking Bart's treasured flesh and me as one.*

My confidence waned because I did not have a backup plan should I have needed to be removed from Bart's quarters in a dire situation. A fireball of energy kicked in and I felt the edge; however, whatever, I could not risk losing that edge. Bart's assurance of me was paramount; my safety was second. Time raced. Everything was in rapid motion. Lynne anxiously awaited as I started into Bart's quarters with the meat. I sat down 60 feet from where Bart rested. He popped up, came fast, hit the brakes, and dropped 1,200 pounds into my lap. His head rested on my chest as he gorged himself on the meat. Bart's behavior toward me was puzzling, but it dispelled many of my fears. I was hesitantly joyful.

While Bart feasted, he swung his left arm over my shoulder and curled it around the back of my neck. I reached for his paw, that formidable paw by which a bear possesses. Touching a paw while eating is an act of trespass rarely forgiven. I worried when he moved to eat a large morsel jammed between his left toes. Then, gently, I stroked his paw with mine. Side by side, our touch glued the trust between us. Between bites, he pressed his cheek against my brow and dipped his head to swallow one last meaningful portion. His right forearm resting beside my knee, with one skilled claw, he speared every small scrap that remained. His breaths ended in long, deep sighs; I, too, sang from my soul.

Then I buried my hands and face in his fur.

River Rapid Romp

We met an aspiring photographer named Fred Donner. He asked if he might visit us in Utah and take photos of our cougars, wolves, and Bart. The photo he had in mind for Bart was a grizzly in a pristine mountain stream in the glow of early morning light.

It was a perfect dawn in early May. The lime green sky was making its way to turquoise. The forecast was for a high of 72°. Newborn leaves were tender, and the mountains held onto their snowy blankets. Bart was in the process of shedding, his legs slick and glossy as otter fur. His winter coat was still full, bleached blond and gold from our high desert sun. Backlit by the morning sun, he glowed in rimfire.

We drove up Mirror Lake Highway to find a perfect spot on the Provo River and pulled Bart's trailer close to the curling water. The light breeze from the river smelled like new-mown hay and watermelon. We set up the safety wire on both sides of the trailer and, in our shorts, waded into the biting cold water. The river's main channel was boiling white with spring runoff.

I told Doug, "We better run some kind of a safety line in front of the rapids."

He replied, "He won't get in those rapids. They're running way too fast."

We opened the trailer and Bart stepped gingerly into the frigid river. Delighted, he raised his legs and floated into the rapids like a giant furry raft. With one last peek over his mountainous hump, he floated around the bend in the river. It was not the time for me to say, "I told you so."

We each grabbed one of Bart's walking chains and a bag of marshmallows and dashed along the rocky bank in frantic pursuit. At the first bend of the river, there he was, waiting for us. Oh, thank God. But as soon as we made eye contact, he bolted back into the rapids and again floated away like a raft with bear ears, checking over his shoulder to make sure we were chasing him.

At the next bend, we saw a fly fisherman fleeing in terror, his waders flapping in the breeze, abandoning an expensive fly rod and gear on the bank. There was no time to explain, even if we could have.

Doug chasing after Bart the Bear in the Provo River.

The river ran wide and slower after the next bend. A log jam glistened, wedged against boulders. Bart clambered aboard for a rest. Now was our chance. Doug and I made our way out into the slower water with chains around our necks and bags of marshmallows in hand.

Doug pulled himself onto the uprooted ponderosa where Bart was perched.

"Come on now! Good boy," he encouraged the grizzly. As if

on cue, Bart bounced on the immense log like a child wildly playing Chopsticks on a piano. The man who had not listened to his wife was pitched backward off the slippery log as Bart did an impressive cannonball back into the main channel. I swear I could see that big grizzly smiling.

Shivering, legs purple, we waded back to shore. Downstream a bit, we saw Bart patiently waiting for us on the bank. He was totally unconcerned with the fisherman 20 yards behind him — he was accustomed to people and had no reason to dislike anyone. Unfortunately, there was no way the angler could have known that. He stood frozen in wide-eyed fright. When he saw two crazed humans draped with chains lunging after a bear, he broke his freeze and escaped into the trees, bonking his head on a low-lying limb.

Reassured of our pursuit, Bart charged back into the river, waiting for us at every bend. By now, we had covered well over a mile. It was an Olympic event.

Slowing and widening, the river was dotted with small islands. By then, Bart was getting as tired as we were. He swam to a patch of green in the shallows. But something was terribly wrong. He looked around and stood very still. Slowly, we waded to the little island. It was blanketed in Canadian thistles, their shiny new leaves glistening with little needles. Bart lifted a front paw, looked at it, and then held it up for us to see. He looked at us with the droopy eyes of a Saint Bernard puppy. He pleaded for sympathy and rescue. Under our breath, we muttered, "You little shithead."

Not pressing our luck, Doug and I approached and gently wrapped his walking chain around his neck as I comforted him with marshmallows. All three of us drenched, we headed to the bank and a stand of Douglas firs.

Bart was happy to be on the soft pine duff of the forest floor; no more sharp, spikey needles in his paws. In fact, the young bear felt spunky — like a dog after a bath. Oh, no! Doug was strong, but no match for the 1,400-pound bear, who kept eyeing the frothing, tossing river 20 yards to our left, clearly planning another delightful plunge.

Totally out of marshmallows, we wrapped one of the chains

around the base of a tall lodgepole pine. Doug attached the snap link of his lead to a chain secured around the pine, and we sat for a moment to gather our wits and breath. We had no choice but to press on. I would tramp through deadfall to find a sturdy tree to wrap my chain around, then Doug and Bart would catch up.

The day grew warmer, and we were grateful for it as it slowly dried our clothes. But it also warmed Bart, who continued to glance at the cool, rumbling river, beckoning him with sparkling crystals as the rapids danced over the rocks. We had to keep moving, but what if he made a mad dash for the river again? At the next anchor point, I had an idea born of desperation. The torturous thistles grew in unruly, spotty patches. I found some close by and used a rock to break them free, yanking the tender young roots from the damp spring soil. I marched up to Bart and bonked him on the top of his head with them ... he remembered. Making our way back through the forest, I kept the chain around my neck and the nasty thistles in my hand.

Now, we both knew but didn't want to say it out loud — that the truck and trailer were on the other side of the river. After what seemed like suspended time and space, we spotted the truck and trailer at the launch spot of the adventure. By then it was midday and the photographer and his assistant were unpacking our picnic lunch. We yelled at them to follow us on their side of the river to where it widened into slower water, and to bring the lunch basket with them. When we reached the slower water, we yelled, "Dump all of the food on the bank!"

With a shudder and a deep breath that was a prayer, we waded back into the numbing runoff. I held tight to the thistles as we headed for the ham and cheese sandwiches, deviled eggs, and ginger snaps dumped on the rocky bank.

"Hold up the bag of cookies and shake them!" we shouted. With a sense of smell two thousand times stronger than a human's, the bear honed in on the warm, spicy scent of ginger and molasses and kept his feet on the rocky bottom. If he had lifted them, we'd have been off on another rapid river romp.

The three of us made landfall and headed to the trailer with rewards of cookies and ham sandwiches. I dropped the thistles, raced to the truck to grab grapes and apples, and chucked them in the trailer. The big bear hopped into the trailer as if nothing had happened and laid down to rest and munch on his grapes.

Doug and I collapsed on the ground. Adrenaline fueled our endurance that day, pushed the limits of our sanity, and proved we may not have any of the latter.
Opening our eyes, we saw our photographer peering down at us. We managed to say, "Gee, Fred, sorry that you didn't get your shot. We'll nail it for you tomorrow."

I didn't need to say anything to Doug about having a safety wire on three sides.

Five for the Road

In a first of its kind for us, we received a call from the *Toronto Star* in Ontario, Canada. The newspaper was sponsoring the Canadian National Sportsmen's Show, which took place in the largest indoor arena in Toronto. They wanted Bart to be the main attraction at the event. They asked us to do a ten-day run with two 20-minute shows a day. Doug and Bart would be in the center of the arena, where Bart would perform some of his "acting" behaviors. I would be on a microphone, narrating about grizzly bears and biology and explaining how we make movies with a grizzly. They offered us a flat fee of $20,000, out of which we were to pay our own gas, food, and lodging.

Heber City to Toronto is just over 2,000 miles. It would take 10 days of roundtrip travel, two to three days to set up and rehearse, plus a 10-day run — that was $869 a day. It would cost $50 a day to have my brother stay at the farm and take care of all the other animals, and we could stay at cheap motels. Still, that left about $800 a day, and it would be an adventure! Of course, we could take our babies, Sausha and Jed, with us. Five for the road.

Our old Dodge truck was still chugging along. We had gone into hock for our 16-foot gooseneck bear trailer. It had a nice tack room that we could load with bear food, grass hay, baby food, dried soups, diapers, and a folding rocking chair. And so, we set off. Jed was ten months old and sat in a car seat in the middle of the two-seat cab of the truck. Sausha, who was still a tiny thing at four, was either in my lap or on a blanket at my feet. We had storybooks and cassette tapes of sing-along children's songs. Four-year-old Bart was approaching 1,400 pounds and was more than okay in his roomy trailer. He enjoyed looking out its windows. He had a better deal than our kids.

We could only make about 400 miles a day, stopping where we could to clean Bart's trailer, change Jed's diaper, and let Sausha stand up and stretch. At night, we would get a motel room with two double beds and let the kids get naked and jump on the beds. I had brought along an electric teakettle so we could make ramen noodles with sandwiches for dinner. Doug would bring me the small rocking chair so I could sing our little ones to sleep. The route took us across Wyoming, Nebraska, Iowa, and Illinois to Michigan. It was a 1982 gas-powered version of an Oregon Trail trip, and it was terrific.

One of the road moments took place in South Chicago. It just happened to be when and where we needed to get gas, and Sausha had to go potty. Being from rural Utah, Sausha and Jed had, sadly, never seen Black people. Neither had Bart. There was not one African American family in Heber City. It had only been two years since the Mormon Church had allowed African American men to hold their priesthood and African American women to enter their temples. Diversity in Utah would take a while.

As it happened, we had pulled off to a gas station in a black neighborhood. I took the kids into the restroom, and when I returned, there was a small crowd gathered around the trailer. Doug had opened the trailer door to water Bart. Three teenage boys were hanging around the trailer windows, and another had made his way toward the top of the trailer to peer down the trailer's roof vent. We surely must have been a strange sight: a man with a big red beard, his family, and an enormous bear drinking out of the gas station water hose. I don't know who was more curious, Bart or his gathering sightseers. "Is that a bear?" "Man, that IS a bear!" Two more boys wanted to crawl on the back of the trailer to get a better look. As I put the kids in the front seat, I heard Doug bringing all the hectic activity under control with an ingenious idea.

"Hey, any of you guys got cigarettes? He likes to crew tobacco." Of course, Bart had never, ever chewed any kind of tobacco. That brought the small crowd off the roof and the sides of the trailer to fish cigarettes out of their packs for Doug to push through the trailer door to Bart, who, come to find out, *did* like to tear the paper off the cigarettes and nibble the tobacco as he looked charmingly back at the smooth, dark faces. There was deep laughter and much good-natured backslapping. At that moment, despite all our differences, we were just people sharing a sense of wonder and awe at another living, breathing, thinking species — momentarily closing any distance between us. I started the truck while Doug secured the trailer and hopped in the cab, calling back to the crowd, "Thanks, guys! See ya'll on the way back!" They all waved goodbye to us like old friends. I tooted the horn back in reply.

Our last stop before crossing the border into Canada was in Detroit. We found a little motel that looked affordable. I went to the window, and the shade pulled up to reveal a barred pass-through window for registration and payment. I thought, "You're not in Kansas anymore, nor Nebraska, nor Utah." The kids were fussing to get out of the cab, and Bart was playing tom-toms on the side of the trailer. We had just released the kids in the freedom of the motel room. Doug was feeding Bart and I was putting on the kettle for our ramen noodle dinner when there was a knock on the door … Oh, no! "There are no bears allowed here," went through my head. It was the owner of the motel, all right. "Say," he said, "I saw your kids, and I was wondering, ah, if maybe you would like to come and have dinner with us, my wife, and our kids. We have some toys."

The kindness of strangers — funny thing, but 30 years later, I still remember the homey creamed chipped beef on toast. It was delicious.

The next morning, we crossed the Canadian border with just our driver's licenses and a letter from the Canadian National Sportsmen's Show stating that the 1,400-pound bear we were hauling was the star of the show. In the ensuing years, we would need a folder of papers the size of a phone book to cross an international border with a grizzly bear in tow. As we pulled into Toronto, we saw big banners advertising the event, with pictures of Bart standing on his hind legs. We entered through the elephant doors of the International Event Center. The massive arena had been there for decades. The arena's managers, Tommy and his son Sean, met us. They had ruddy cheeks and thick Irish brogues. Encircling the outside of the arena were hundreds of booths featuring everything from ATVs to hiking socks — everything to do with the outdoors.

There was a roped-off place for the truck and Bart's trailer. A cubicle under a cement stairwell was our dressing room. Our sponsors from the *Toronto Star* were there to greet us. We stayed at a small hotel not far away, and Sean would drive us back and forth so we could leave the truck attached to the trailer. One of the newspaper folks had arranged for his niece to watch over Jed and Sausha while we rehearsed and performed. We checked out the 12,000-seat arena where we were to do our 20-minute shows. The floor of the arena was covered ankle-deep in oak and sycamore leaves and chunks of bark, some with wood mushrooms still attached. They must have raked every hardwood forest within ten miles to gather the leaves. The smell was earthy and damp, with just a hint of smoke and burnt sugar. A big part of the show was the retriever trials, with champion bird dogs from all over Canada. The trials took place just before our performance — there were lots of messages for Bart's giant olfactory system in all those leaves. Good thing Bart liked dogs.

Our rehearsals went well. We had improvised a script that focused on the biology and legends of the grizzly bear. We had Bart perform some of his most charming behaviors, including holding his teddy bear. Then Doug would tumble about with him, and at the end with the music's crescendo, Bart would rise to all of his 10 feet, and I would say, "Ladies and Gentlemen, the magnificent Kodiak." Then he would wave bye-bye and exit to his trailer. Standing upright is not a natural posture for a bear. Sure, they stand up in the wild, but generally, just for a few seconds to get a better view of their surroundings. After he learned to hit a mark, standing upright was the next skill Bart mastered, and it earned him the most applause.

We were all having a great time, including the kids. On the opening day of the show, I remember feeling the energy as we pulled the trailer into the arena. Egad! The place was packed! Every seat was taken, and the fire marshal had closed the doors. Twelve thousand people were focused on us. We had better be good.

Bart the Bear performing at the Canadian National Sportsmen's Show in 1982.

The show went beautifully. At the end of the first performance, I could see Bart react to the resounding applause; his eyes sparkled, he put a zip in his behaviors, and stood even taller at the end of the performance.

At the second show, Bart bounced out of his trailer to another full house seated 360 degrees around him. He turned in a circle as if to make eye contact with everyone on the packed bleachers. He pranced through his performance, and when we gave him his teddy bear to hold, the crowd roared with adoration. At that moment, I believe something clicked in his huge head; Bart understood star power.

He started to make up his own routine. Instead of just holding the toy bear, he took it by the ear with his front teeth and whirled it in circles above his head. The crowd laughed and whistled. I tried to cover for his antics on the microphone, "Bart, you be nice to your teddy bear."

Then, as if on cue, he swatted his stuffed bear across the arena like a soccer ball. Doug took possession of the battered toy as we moved to the final scene. He performed with gusto, but when Doug asked him to exit stage left to his trailer, he instead paraded around the arena smiling at the crowd (yes, bears do smile). Oh no, what in the hell do we do? Doug and I exchanged a look. Pretending it to be part of the show, Doug interrupted Bart's curtain call with a hug but secretly bit him on the ear, whispering, "You get in, NOW." That could've gone really bad. Bart reluctantly strolled to his trailer. That was when we knew that Bart was a Ham, A Glory Hog, a Scene-Stealer, a Rock Star!

After that, we went back to basic training. Every behavior we ask of the bears or any of our animals, including our dogs, is positively reinforced. Sit, come, stay — all the commands are rewarded with treats and affection. Pretty simple stuff. For the bigger predators — bears, wolves, cougars — there is one command they must obey for their own safety and that of everyone around — the command "IN." One cannot just grab these big guys by the collar and haul them away for the day. In the event of the unexpected — fire, flood, high winds, the lights go out, the set walls fall over, the cameraman has a heart attack (that has happened) — the animal must load when it is commanded. Without this control, we would have no business being in the business.

That evening, after the show had closed for the night, we asked Tommy, Sean, and as many insiders from the newspaper as we could muster to stay with us in the arena We brought Bart back out into the fully-lit arena. Bart had some fun, but that time Doug told him to go in and then did the top bear display — yelling, stomping, pounding the ground, charging, baring his teeth, and growling. Bart remembered and understood that loading was obligatory. For the rest of the show, he did so on cue.

It was a good thing, too, for on his final performance, the people from the *Toronto Star*, who had been very good to us, asked if Miss Toronto might have her picture taken with Bart, with her hometown cheering on. "Okay, well ... Sure ... I guess?" So, in the last moments of the show, the announcer took the microphone and said, "Ladies and gentlemen, Laura Mahoney, Miss Toronto!" A glamorous young woman walked into the arena in a full-length fur coat and spiked heels. No one had said anything about a fur coat! She sashayed up to Doug and Bart, struck a pose, and whipped off the fur coat to reveal a string bikini clinging to ample curves. She tossed her hair, put one hand behind her head, stuck her hip out, and offered her other hand to Bart. I honestly don't know who was more stunned, Doug, me, Bart, or Miss Toronto, when Bart offered his huge paw in return, and she lost her balance and did a butt-plant. The audience laughed and applauded.

Doug and I exchanged a powerful, two-second look. Doug instantly told Bart to load, and I brought up the rear. We secured the latch and exchanged another two-second glance that said, "Oh my God, what if ... How stupid could we be? We would never take a chance like that again, never." How much we needed to learn, but for now ... thank God! Miss Toronto was helped back into her fur coat as she waved to the crowd. "All's well that ends well" held a new meaning for us.

The kind Canadians helped us pack up with fresh hay and feed for Bart, new books and sing-along cassette tapes for the kids, and a big box of Canadian back bacon. We took I-90 through Buffalo, New York, on the way home and stopped in Erie, Pennsylvania, to see Grandpa Ray and Grandma Jean Seus. We backed the trailer into their narrow driveway, where it fit snugly against the back doorsteps — so close that we could look Bart in the eye from the kitchen of Doug's boyhood home. Long-time neighbors, old friends, and the *Erie Times* newspaper reporter all came calling. The boy who had gone West was back for a day or two with his wife, his kids, and a three-quarter-ton bear.

After our time with Jean and Ray, we made it back to our home in the mountains. We'd had a wonderful adventure while learning some important lessons. Things were going our way. We actually had our first savings account. Life was as sweet and golden as apple pie. Then came a knock at the door.

A Knock at the Door

Bright yellow leaves were fluttering to the ground like butterflies, and the sky was the electric blue of mid-October. I answered the door. It was Jack Perry, our neighbor from two roads over. Sausha was in preschool with his daughter. His wife, Rose, and I often carpooled our little girls together. Today, Jack was in his police uniform, his gold buttons and badge glinting against the navy blue fabric like aspen leaves in the sun. He held papers in his hand and looked apologetic.

"Hi, Jack. What is it? I mean … is everything okay?" I stammered.

"I'm sorry, Lynne, I have to serve this summons to you and Doug. You'll have to sign for it."

"Oh, well, sure, I guess, sure … Do you have time to come in for a cup of coffee?" He sucked in one of his cheeks, did not smile, and looked down at his badge with a deep sigh.

"Oh, yeah, of course not," I said, "Sure." I signed at the date and time stamp and took the papers to the kitchen table. The lawsuit had been filed by our next-door neighbor, Mrs. Henry, a middle-aged woman with three ex-husbands. She worked at the county courthouse. We were well acquainted with her, as she had often come uninvited through the front gate of our property to show her boyfriends and relatives our animals. And more than once, Doug had pulled her car out of deep snowbanks.

It had been four years since Wasatch County had granted us

> # A summary of the summons received from the District Court of Wasatch County
>
> ### COUNT 1
> ZONING VIOLATION of the RA-2 Residential Agricultural Zone. Such zone permitted the care and keeping of domestic animals and fowl for personal use, but not for sale or barter.
>
> ### COUNT 2
> NUISANCE
> The animals are a dangerous hazard and could escape and attack the plaintiff at any time of the day or night. The animals howl and disturb the plaintiff's tranquility and interfere with her enjoyment of life. As a direct result of the said Defendants' use of their property, the plaintiff has sustained damages in the amount of $100,000.00
>
> ### COUNT 3
> FAILURE TO ENFORCE DEVELOPMENT CODE
> The plaintiff demands the immediate removal of the Seus animals and that failure to do so would compromise the health, safety, and morals of the county. Therefore, Wasatch County should be ordered to pay her attorney fees, court costs, and an additional relief of $100,000.

building permits and variances that expressly allowed bear cages, wolf runs, and eight-foot-high fences. The neighbors, including Mrs. Henry, had received written notice of the request for the variances and permits and had been present at an onsite visit from the Wasatch County Board of Adjustments and the county planner. None of the neighbors had expressed any objections. In fact, Mrs. Henry had given us a handwritten note saying she had no objections. Four years later, that bitter woman was suing us and also Wasatch County for approving building permits for our animal enclosures.

The zoning code allowed the care and keeping of domestic animals. Our variances expressly stated bear cages and wolf runs. Now, Mrs. Henry was in a state of disturbed tranquility — "in fear for her life" — and $100,000 would make her feel safer. She also demanded that the animals immediately be removed from the property.

It would take a year for the ordeal to end — a year of uncertainty, anxiety, worry, sleepless nights, gut ache, and deep debt. A year that should have been full of watching our son, Jed, take his first baby steps and our little daughter start preschool. There was a mantra stuck in my head: "Follow your bliss, your preposterous dream." So, we thought we were going to start from nothing, gather a wolf pack, rescue denned and doomed varmints, take in orphaned deer, get a giant bear, have a family, and build a future — well, you're goddamn right we are!

Mrs. Henry's niece confided to us that she had run into "a big gun lawyer" who was eager to share in the prize money. The county had its own attorney on staff; we would have to get a legal team of our own for relying on the county's written permission to build bear cages and wolf runs. We also had to show that our animals were "for the use of man," which is the definition of domestic. We used what savings we had and remortgaged our house to retain an A-list law firm from Salt Lake City and entered a long, cold season of uncertainty.

The first thing the law firm did was to petition the judge in the Fourth District Court to dismiss the case as frivolous. He would not. Our lawyers then asked the judge to recuse himself because he knew the plaintiff well and worked with her at the small courthouse in Heber City. He would not.

We pleaded not guilty and demanded a trial by jury.

Then it started: disclosures, depositions, research, conference calls, trial preparation, subpoenas of county officials and neighbors, affidavits, jury selection, memos, and motions. In addition to that, we found ourselves paying for photocopies, long-distance phone calls, mileage, and lunch for lawyers when we could barely feed ourselves. It took eight months for our case to go to trial. I spent week after week at the BYU Microfilm Library, researching the history of Wasatch County zoning codes to help save on the attorney's research costs. I resented every minute. I would've given anything just to be with my babies, my bears, my wolves — my family.

Finally, in July, our three-day jury trial arrived. By day three, it was being covered by four newspapers and two Salt Lake City TV stations. Our neighbors, the same neighbors who had stood in quiet shock and surprise as we had settled onto the banks of Daniels Creek five years earlier, were now subpoenaed to be witnesses. They took the stand, were sworn in, testified, and were cross-examined. I don't believe any of them had ever been in a court of law before. One by one, they testified:

"No, I'm not scared for me and my family. They have their own little kids down there with their animals."

"No, the wolf howls don't bother me; we like to hear them."

"No, the bears don't scare us; we love to go down to visit them."

"They have federal inspectors there all the time checking out their cages and fences, just like the Hogle Zoo in Salt Lake."

"No, their animals have never been running around the neighborhood."

"The animals aren't hurting anyone. Doug and Lynne are good people, and besides, they cleaned up that old place real nice. Best damn neighbors I ever had."

The jury retired for deliberation. Doug and I went across the street to the local drug store soda fountain with the legal team. I remember staring at the bubbles in my root beer float, watching them float to the top like a metaphor — stay on top, stay on top, even if, even if. The bubbles were still floating when a neighbor ran in and said, "Jury is back." It had been just 20 minutes.

We entered the courthouse and were reseated. I could hear my heart in my ears. The jury had ruled in our favor on all twelve of the questions that had been put to them. Most importantly, we should be able to rely on the variances and building permits issued to us by Wasatch County, and our animals were, by their very use,

Happy scenes from our life with animals. Clockwise from top: Jack the black bear with Jed and Sausha; Sausha with Skeeter the fox; Jed and me with Billy the Badger.

domestic. Mrs. Henry was not entitled to any damages from anyone, and she would be liable for the court costs. With every word the jury foreman read, the judge's jaw clenched harder, harder, and harder; his mouth pressed into a hard, black line like that of a turtle. The gavel slammed like a hammer on a horseshoe, "Court adjourned."

A neighbor stood and shouted, arms overhead, "God lives!" It was over.

But it was not over.

The next day, the judge overturned the jury's verdict. Our animals were not, in his juristic opinion, domestic. We stood in criminal violation of the zoning code, and the county could press criminal charges against us. We must get rid of our animals in 30 days or face six months in jail. It was not over; it started over.

Our attorneys petitioned the court for more time to find a resolution and relocate the animals, if necessary. After all, it was now a criminal case, and a family's livelihood was at stake. Where were we supposed to go? The rebuilding of a facility that met USDA shelter requirements for the animals would take another four years and require a great cash outlay, cash we did not have. We pleaded for mercy from the court; we had had no criminal intent or malice. We were given a grace period of 90 days.

There was only one way to keep us and our animals in our home: change the zoning code. The county planner, who had signed and issued the building permits, was dead set against spot zoning and dug in his heels. The county attorney agreed with him and turned on us like a stepped-on rattler. Our animals must go. Ninety days.

That time, the whole valley took up our case. Most everyone outside the city limits was also zoned RA-2, and many were in technical violation of the zoning code by selling hay and eggs. The war was on, not just for us. If the county could rescind *our* building permits, what about *theirs*? Their barns, corrals, chicken coops, fences?

There were legal petitions to change the zoning code on every store counter in town. Only the county commissioners could do so. We requested a place on the agenda at the next commissioner's meeting six weeks away. It was a long six weeks, but thank God for those six weeks. The word "zoning" buzzed, hissed, spat, raged, rumbled, and roared all over the county. Signs appeared on homemade poster boards all over town.

"Don't Take Our Bear!" "If You Care, Be There!" "How is *Your* Building Permit Today?"

The local weekly paper, *The Wasatch Wave*, had to add four extra pages for six weeks to accommodate the letters to the editor. Every one of them was on our behalf. By the day of the meeting, on a cold February afternoon, the cars and trucks circled around the courthouse for blocks. The place was so packed that two extra sheriff deputies were called in. One of our cowboy neighbors brought a rope turned into a noose. Voices were full of flint and steel and gunpowder.

At that time, Salt Lake City had only three TV stations. All three of them were there. To our community, it felt like everyone's personal freedom and property rights were at stake. The county attorney was booed off the floor. The county planner was blocked at the door by people standing shoulder to shoulder like so many boulders. "Order! Order!" the deputies commanded. The public comments shook the walls like storm waves. It was obvious that the re-zoning of the entire valley was never going to be resolved in a single meeting. It would take countless meetings, public notices, committees, lawyers, local ballots, and many months. We were down to 42 days.

Then, a small, red-headed grandmother made her way to the commissioner's table. It was Sister Mable McFee, chairwoman of the valley's Republican Party and president of our valley's Mormon Relief Society. She placed a motion before the board that the zoning from the beginning to the end of Little Sweden Road, including the back hills, be immediately spot-zoned to allow for "the care and keeping of animals for sale or barter." The word "domestic" was removed — it was decided that an animal is an animal. Period. End of story.

In front of half the town, three TV cameras, and four newspaper reporters, the commissioners passed the motion five to two. A roar rang out that could be heard outside the building. The county planner took cover down a hallway. An hour later, the local beer bar was just about as packed as the courthouse had been with joyous revelers. It was a grasp, however small, at true democracy and the

Western way of life.

It was finally over.

To this day there is a small, bright red rectangle on the Heber Valley Zoning Map. These neighbors had proved to be the best of friends. That has never changed.

Dear Editor,

To: The People of Wasatch County,

We would like to thank you, the many people who have tried so hard to help us. Last Friday's 2 P.M. meeting was held at a time when men had to take off work, most women had to find babysitters, and many cars were too frozen to start. And yet, there were over 300 of you standing shoulder to shoulder in the commissioner's chambers and lined up and down the halls and stairways. It is obvious that this zoning situation goes far beyond our particular case. But, how truly grateful we must be to live in a country where we can come before our leaders, as we did, and more importantly that through the precious freedoms we enjoy, freedom of the press, freedom of speech, freedom to assemble, there is a way for the people to tackle and solve problems that exist in our valley. To our neighbors who have treated us like family, to our friends who have shared all our turmoil and anxiety, to the people we don't even know who started petitions and called to ask to help, you will never know how deeply you have touched our hearts. No matter what the future holds for our animals and us, we will never forget that we lived amidst a proud and spirited people. Thank you and God bless you.

Sincerely,

Doug and Lynne Seus

Climbing Out of "Setback Canyon"

With our hard-won victory, we started climbing out of "setback canyon." We weren't starting over; that would've been easier with just Doug and me and a wolf belaying each other up and over. Now there were two little kids and thirty-five wild animals, one of which was a 1,400-pound bear that we were also pulling up and out.

We hounded the Utah Film Commission and every advertising agency in the state. We worked each and every job we could find. There were day jobs for skunks, raccoons, porcupines, owls, bald eagles, sheep, parakeets, dogs, cats, horses, snakes, and Madagascar cockroaches (yes, there is a secret way to get a cockroach to crawl on an exact path over someone's body).

We did low-budget independent films. One was so micro-low budget that they only had a small household generator to light the night scene. Doug was in a bearskin robe playing a Viking berserker wrestling Bart. The generator failed. Everyone stood frozen in the total darkness of a new moon. What does one do with a huge bear that can't see his half-naked trainer or the way to his trailer? Doug had had a feeling that the rickety generator might fail — and the foresight to have the small crew pull their cars onto the field, facing the scene. People fumbled to reach their vehicles. Eureka! The car headlamp lighting was better than the puny generator, and the end product on film was wonderfully eerie.

For years, there were dozens of these hand-to-mouth jobs, and most all have stories to tell, but a few perch prominently on the ledges of our climb back up.

~~~~~~~~~~~~~~~~~~~~~~~~~

Pink Chiffon and Pig Shit

I sourced an advertising agency that needed six baby pigs for a still product photo. The ad featured two utterly adorable four-year-old girls in white lace and chiffon dresses with pink satin sashes. They were to be seated against a white backdrop among big, beautifully wrapped, pink-and-white gift boxes, from which would emerge the piglets. Each of the little girls was to hold a baby pig on her lap while staring wide-eyed and unsmiling into the camera, beribboned ringlets tumbling about her shoulders. The little pigs had to be pink to match the scene. The pay was $50 a pig — $300 for the day. We would find a way.

We knew that the fellow who came by to read our gas meter owned pigs near Salt Lake City. Perfect timing; he had a litter of two-week-old, pink piglets. We could borrow them for a day in exchange for crates of Pippin apples from one of the old trees by our pioneer cabin. Terrific! He would have them ready for us the morning of the shoot.

True to his word, when we arrived at his place, we found a cardboard box with six little piglets. Only one problem: they were covered with gritty brown pig poop and slop. We didn't want to make the guy feel like, well … a pig farmer or something, so we just put the box in the car and headed for the photo studio.

Our call was in less than an hour. We thought we would be able to get the piglets under a hose, or at least into a restroom sink. What luck! There was a spigot with a hose on the lawn outside the studio. I grabbed my hairbrush from my purse. Doug held the little guys under their front legs while I hosed and brushed. The experience of their first bath stimulated the little oinkers; they squirted forest-green piglet poop all over Doug while I scrubbed. Then I hosed Doug off as best I could. We moved into the studio with squeaky-clean, squealing piggies and Doug, soaking wet and covered from neck to shoes in ... you know what ... he smelled like ... you know what ... he looked like ... you know what. I thought it was hysterically funny. Doug was totally pissed off — but mainly he was pissed on. He can laugh about it now, a little bit.

~~~~~~~~~~~~~~~~~~~~~~~~~~~~

Mr. Krueger's Christmas

That Christmas, we used our calico cat, Sally, for a Christmas special called *Mr. Krueger's Christmas*. Produced by Bonneville Productions and directed by our pal, Kieth Merrill, it starred Jimmy Stewart (Yes, Jimmy Stewart!). The story was about an elderly widower who survives a lonely Christmas with his cat, his daydreams, and a nativity scene. When we arrived on set, Mr. Stewart came over to us and said, as only he could have said it, "Well now, let me meet my co-star." He scooped up the cat, and we followed him to a quiet corner. He and Doug spoke in whispery voices, not about the cat, but of their shared military service. An Air Force major general and an Army private. The general spoke of the death of his son, killed in action in Vietnam. Ron would have been about Doug's age. All the while, he tenderly stroked Sally. I sat on the cat crate with my back turned to them, far enough away so as to not hear clearly but close enough to be their sentry. It was a sacred conversation, privy only to warriors. I held my post until Mr. Stewart and Sally were called to set.

~~~~~~~~~~~~~~~~~~~~~~~~~~~~

How Cold is Cold?

The next call came from BBC Canada. The script was Farley Mowat's classic, *Lost in the Barrens*. Being fans of Mowat's work, we

Bart the Bear on the set of *Lost in the Barrens*.

were excited at the prospect of being part of one of his stories on film. It was right after Christmas, and we were housebound, with no jobs in sight. We gladly took off and headed for the Hudson Bay area, 100 miles north of Winnipeg, Canada.

Our first clue came in North Dakota. The wind blew sideways, stabbing ice picks through our heavy coats and boots. Bart's trailer was filled with grass hay as bedding and insulation, but the cold and the snow blowing through expanded-metal trailer windows rimmed his ears in hoarfrost. Like wolverine and wolf fur, bear fur is not supposed to frost. It did. It was that cold.

We stopped at the small town of Casselton, not far from Fargo, where we found a general store that was just about to close. They had plywood in stock. The kind owners let us pull into their garage, where our fingers would bend. They helped us drill holes in the plywood and wire the wooden sheets to the window vents of the trailer. That helped with the frost on Bart's ears, but every time Doug stepped out of the truck, his beard and eyebrows would instantly turn white with frost. We crawled through the snow and screaming wind of the high prairie and arrived two days late at the production office in Winnipeg. The temperature was 45° below. The weatherproof Canadians, with cheeks as red and hard as Jonathan apples, informed us that we would not be filming until it warmed up; the camera cables were too frozen to be unrolled.

The crew sent us north, toward Hudson Bay, to a forest lodge run by a Newfoundland family. A set of small cabins clustered around a frozen lake, which was used for fishing and canoeing during the short summer. The mother and her grown sons greeted us at the main lodge with steaming English meat pies and Canadian beer. Heaven at 45° below. The walk from the lodge back to the cabins required ski masks, woolen mittens, scarves, hats, and Sorel boots on snowshoes. It was hard to sleep worrying about Bart. Even with the extra hay and boarded windows, I knew he was cold.

A knock on the door at dawn. It was a message brought by one of the apple-cheeked people. It had warmed up — it was only 30° below — and we would be filming today. I learned some things about filming at 30° below: don't wear mascara because your eyelashes freeze solid and break off, and don't drink coffee because the warmth in your belly is not worth the effort of taking six layers off your butt to pee in an unheated outhouse. I also learned a lesson in nonverbal, interspecies communication.

We were filming on a frozen lake. All of Bart's usual treats — meat cuts, apples, grapes, and cookies — were frozen solid. We had asked the mom at the lodge to make us up a big granite pot full of beef stew. Production had found us a sturdy propane stove to keep the stew from freezing, but it froze around the rim of the pot anyway. Only the middle core of the stew stayed unfrozen long enough for us to ladle a scoop into Bart's feed pan. We also had to keep the feed pan close to the propane burner to keep it from freezing. We didn't want to risk Bart's tongue sticking to the frozen metal.

The scene called for two boys to be "lost in the barrens" and run into a hungry grizzly bear. Bart was, as usual, doing his brilliant job of acting: going to his mark, striking out with his paw, standing up, and roaring his silent roar. He suddenly stopped acting — stopped cold. He sat down close to Doug, lifted his upper body in his "beg-up" position, and held out a giant forefoot, paw outward. Then, looking Doug directly in the eye, he stretched his paw straight out, inches from Doug's face. When Doug stood speechless, Bart thrust his paw even further forward, gently touching Doug's face. "Do you not see my feet are freezing?" asked the bear. Bart's eyes locked with Doug's. Without taking his eyes from Bart's, Doug said, "Cut! We are taking a break. Bart says his paws are cold." Doug took Bart back to the hay in his trailer. He laid him on his side and rubbed his paws like a father with a small son whose feet are cold. After a bit, Bart rolled over and laid his head in Doug's lap.

We told the director that Bart was finished for the day. The director thanked us heartily and assured us that he had every shot he needed. Besides, he said, the actors were also too bone-cold to continue. As I stood by the trailer, I heard Doug say softly, "I'm sorry, Bart. We are going home now." And we did.

~~~~~~~~~~~~~~~~~~~~~~~~~~

Badger by the Balls

Periodically, the United States Postal Service issues stamps featuring the work of wildlife artists. In 1981, there was a "Save Our Wildlife Habitat" series. We were nervously thrilled when we received a call from EUE/Screen Gems Ltd. The studio was producing four commercials featuring the stamps for a prestigious advertising agency out of New York City. Now we were playing with the big boys. The concept was simple: film live-action of the wild animal depicted on the stamp, and when the action of the animal matched the artist's rendition, snap a freeze-frame that turns into the stamp. It was a clever concept, but totally ass-backwards. It would have been so much easier to shoot the action footage first, then have the artist work from a freeze-frame. But it was what it was, and we were grateful for the work.

Fortunately, we had two of the four wild animals called for: a grizzly in a mountain setting and a badger in grassland. The other two stamps called for a yearling black bear in a burnt tree and mallard ducks in wetlands. Our own black bear, Jack, was too big to match the young bear on the stamp. We would find and coordinate a young black bear and the ducks.

The grizzly coming to a mark with snow-covered mountains in the background was a piece of cake in our own backyard with Bart. And Billy the Badger, the little sofa pillow with legs that had lived behind the toilet, had grown into a proud and handsome badger man. He continued to think people's ankles were great fun, but I was his favorite person and could still tickle his tummy. I could even pick him up if I grabbed a handful of his creamy belly fur with one hand and the back of his neck with the other so he couldn't bite me. Billy didn't really like Doug much, probably because he spent all his time with a certain Kodiak bear. Being the lucky, favored one, I popped Billy into a dog crate, checked him as baggage, and flew from Salt Lake City to Topeka, Kansas. I vividly remember him hissing and stomping at anyone who looked into the dog crate to see what kind of cute little puppy was inside. The crate rocked away down the luggage conveyor belt. He was still hissing and stomping when I picked him up at the baggage claim in Topeka.

The badger footage would be filmed in the Flint Hills of Kansas at the National Tall Grass Prairie Preserve. I rented a car and drove to the preserve. Even though I was born of the prairie, until that moment, I'd had no idea what the endless acres, now covered with corn and wheat, looked like in their natural state to the original Pawnee and Kanza people. The native grass was over my head; an elk could disappear in it. The prairie moved like an ocean, a living being with a spirit. I had a sudden, strong impulse to take off my clothes and swim through the waving green sea.

The arrival of the camera crew and the voice of the director snapped me back into the moment. The art director had found a location that resembled the stamp. I think it was an old buffalo wallow. It only took a few shovels of dirt to rearrange the ground and make it look like the badger den on the stamp. In the artist's rendition, the badger was emerging from his den, looking to the left. Unlike Bart, Billy was not trained to hit a mark. We had only been in the business a few years, and we had a lot to learn. However, I could get him into the den mound and hold on to him by his belly fur so he would stay put. I took Billy with me and crawled inside the makeshift den. I scrunched myself down inside and positioned Billy, keeping a hold on his belly. Then, I heard the director say, "Okay, shoot." Then I heard, "Cut, cut, cut!"

"Lynne," he called, "we can see the top of your head and your arm." The art director came to the rescue, and I disappeared behind five sacksful of peat moss. "One more thing, Lynne, Billy needs to be moved forward about six inches." There was only one place I could hold onto Billy so he would be far enough forward. I gently slid my hand back to find two convenient furry little knobs to hang onto. Billy snorted, but he held still. "Maybe he likes it," I thought. At that moment, the clouds cleared, matching exactly the sky in the stamp. "Got it! Great!" called the director. I dug peat moss out of my ears all the way back to Utah.

~~~~~~~~~~~~~~~~~~~~~~~~~~~

Killer the Bear's Dad

For the black bear scene, the agency had scouted locations in the riparian countryside just south of Savannah, Georgia. It was long before the days of the Internet. A friend of a friend in the bear world told us there was a guy in the Southeast who had a yearling black bear. The bear's owner sounded okay over the phone, so Doug and I hopped on a plane to Atlanta, rented a car, and met him in Savannah.

He showed up right on time, with the black bear sitting beside him in the cab of an old Chevy truck. Donny's black eyes were set just a little too deep for comfort. Coarse, black hair extended from his head and down over his neck and arms to almost completely cover his pale skin. When he stepped out of the truck, we noticed his hands reached to the top of his knees. He looked inhumanly strong.

"Hi, I'm Donny, and this is Killer; he's my son." The bear had the gentle, amber eyes of a Cocker Spaniel. We asked about a pen for the bear. "Hell no, I don't need no pen! Killer sleeps with me." Even though we had rented a couple of pet-friendly rooms at a Courtyard Marriott, there was no persuading the manager to let the bear share Donny's bed. We agreed that Killer would spend the night in the cab of the Chevy truck with a couple of Marriott pillows and blankets.

Just as we were drifting off to sleep about midnight, we heard a hysterical, high-pitched voice. "Killer! God Damn it, Killer! Come back here! God Damn It, Killer!" We looked out the window of our room, which faced the hotel's pool, to see Killer having a wonderful time being crazy and wild in the illuminated blue water. Every time Donny was about to catch him, the young bear would splash and dash to the other side of the pool. Then, in an insane frenzy, Donny ripped the Coke machine off the wall and ran it toward Killer like a battering ram. When Killer saw that his "dad" had turned into a Coke machine, he jumped out of the pool and disappeared into the dimly lit parking lot.

Still trying to pull on our jeans, Doug and I followed Donny, who had traded the Coke machine for a newspaper stand to bludgeon Killer. As we turned the corner, we saw a well-dressed businessman getting his luggage out of the back seat of his sedan. Out of the darkness, a 100-pound black bear dove over his back, seeking refuge in his car. The poor guy turned around to see a berserk man holding a newspaper stand over his head, charging after the bear, who was now scared shitless in the back of the stranger's car.

With Killer trapped into submission, we tried desperately to explain things to the quivering businessman. Donny put down the newspaper stand and told us he would spend the rest of the night holding onto Killer in the cab of his truck. We returned to the courtyard to see our New York producer, the client, and the director standing semi-clothed outside their rooms in total bewilderment. We just cleared our throats, smiled, and said, "Good night, see you in the morning."

The first shot the next morning was the mallard ducks in their wetland habitat. The director had found a lovely, swampy pond with the same reeds and cattails as the artwork on the stamp — with the addition of golf-ball-size, yellow eyeballs, with devilish, elliptical pupils, floating just above the pond surface. I reassured myself that these alligators would most likely stay in place guarding their nests.

We had sourced a local bird farm that had mallards. Donny had come along early to help us wrangle the ducks. (The bear shot wasn't up until the late afternoon; Killer was locked in the truck with a security guard standing by.) We arrived at the bird farm, and the owner led us past pens of golden pheasants, sage grouse, Chukar partridge, and Gambel's quail on the way to the pen that held the mallards.

The drakes were stunning, with their forest green, opalescent heads. The hens were a sweet, soft brown. We asked to buy five pairs. The owner said he would go get the key for the padlock on the pen. "Don't worry 'bout no damn key!" whooped Donny in midair as he executed a precise Karate kick that took out the lock, hinge, and door frame of the pen. "Ah, umm, well, we will pay for that too," I said, as Doug and I exchanged a what-the-hell-have-we-gotten-into look. We loaded the ducks, pair-by-pair, in separate crates and drove back to the shoot location.

The mallards were as tame as barnyard ducks, but it was going to be a matter of pure luck to get them to fly past the camera in any semblance of the stamp's image. The plan was for me to be on the bow of a rented rowboat on one end of the pond and release a pair of ducks to fly cross-camera to Doug, who was standing beside another boat with a duck call, cracked corn, and a big dip net. We went for the shot, knowing it would take several releases to match the stamp's art with the drake flying slightly ahead of his hen. After a couple of takes, the ducks got the idea of that A to B flight pattern, but an unforeseen problem presented itself. As the birds landed for the corn, they swam in circles so fast they were almost impossible to catch for the next take. Suddenly, Donny called out loudly to everyone. "I got an idea; just cut 'em webs out between 'em's little feet, and that'll slow 'em down!"

A moment of dead silence. Donny looked at the stunned director and client, "Well … them gators gotta eat too!" then he hee-hawed a laugh an octave higher than his voice. The producer looked at us in horror. Doug mustered a laugh and said, "Oh, he's just kidding, aren't you, Donny?!" poking him under the water with the net handle.

With several more takes, the ducks, webs intact and gullets full, slowed down enough to be netted. We landed a great freeze-frame.

On to the moment we were dreading — the black bear shot. The scene called for the young bear to climb up a fire-blackened tree, stop at an exact spot, and look toward the camera. Doug had designed an ingenious prop tree to match the stamp. Out of the camera's view, he built little paw holds and a small seat where the bear was supposed to stop and look. Now, Killer was the sweetest little bear you could ever hope to see, but he had absolutely no training whatsoever. We had the idea to use candy gummy worms as bait. If they showed on camera, we hoped they would just look natural. We showed Killer where the gummy worms were and had the cameras roll.

Wow! Up the tree he went and right to his perch, ate a gummy worm, and looked out to us. Perfect on the first take! The director called for one more take for safety. Again, perfect!

Donny was so elated that he started running around and whooping like a crazed chimp. In his joy, he employed his kickboxing moves to knock over tree stumps. Suddenly, he stopped and began tearing off his clothes, screaming, "Oh shit, oh shit, oh shit!" He had kicked over a stump that was home to a red ant nest. He slapped madly at the tiny bits of red venom that were embedded in the wiry black hair covering his body. I led him away, kicking and screaming in his Speedo, to the pond while Doug led the gentle black bear to the truck. Once again, the producer, client, and crew just stood in slack-jawed amazement.

That night, back at the hotel, I heard Doug roaring with laughter so hard in the shower it echoed down the halls. When he stepped out of the shower, even the towel he was drying his hair with could not muffle his huge laugh. We just looked at each other and laughed 'till we cried. What else was there to do? Another unexpected lesson: always meet subcontracted trainers in advance and in person.

~~~~~~~~~~~~~~~~~~~~~~~~~~~~

The Gambler

Our whole family danced around the house when the call came to take Bart to Arizona for *The Gambler: The Adventure Continues*. I can still hear the song in my head, "You've got to know when to hold 'em, know when to fold 'em ..." Kenny Rogers played Brady Hawkes, the gambler, and Bruce Boxleitner played Billy Montana.

Our location was Sedona, Arizona, on the Verde River. We settled Bart among the piñon pines, standing like guardians at attention among the medieval castles of red rock. We were familiar with red rock country — the red rock of Southern Utah starts to unfold just three and a half hours from our home in the alpine meadows of the Wasatch Range. The national park roads there are often bumper-to-bumper with tourist traffic. That is why our family would seek out and hike the game trails that sneak through the yucca and silver buffalo brush growing beneath stacked crimson towers. The prehistoric red rock layer cake is a geologist's dream.

Yet, that landscape was different — the rock wasn't red; it was bright orange, and it glowed. Strangely, even the silence felt different. We always travel with a heavy canvas bag of reference books. I could not help reaching for the thick, worn geology book. I needed to understand that verdant land.

There is a Supai Group of sedimentary rocks that were deposited in Utah about 270 million years ago during the Permian Period, but the Schenbly Hill Formation of that group, with its frosted grains of quartz stained by hematite (iron oxide), is primarily found in Sedona. I searched through the bag, and at the bottom was a volume on the archeology of the Puebloan culture. As part of that Puebloan history, the Sinagua people occupied the area from approximately A.D. 600 to 1400. However, the ruins of these people are found only on the outskirts of Sedona. Archeologists surmise that Sedona's townsite had been a ceremonial center. The shining orange formations are millions of years old. The piñon trees are deep green with life renewing itself. The atmosphere was singular and incomprehensible — a wave of energy, both foreign and familiar, tapped me on the shoulder. I wondered if Bart felt it, too.

But it was time to work. The story is set in the year 1890. Brady Hawkes, his 12-year-old son, Jeremiah, and their pal, Billy Montana, are aboard a train bound for a world-class gambling event in San Francisco, as is the owner of the railroad. The tycoon travels in his private car with gilded windows, mahogany tables, and scarlet velvet drapes. He and his partner are sipping champagne with their beautiful wives. Out of nowhere, a vicious, dirty, rotten band of bad guys jump the train and blast bullets through the engine. The train comes to a screeching halt, and everyone on board is thrown from their seats. The villains hold the white-haired tycoon at gunpoint and demand to know where the gold is. The railroad boss has been robbed before, and the gold is on a stagecoach headed to Bristol, Arizona, 300 miles away. Enraged, the no-good ruffians grab Jeremiah, hold a machete to his throat, and demand a million dollars be waiting for them in Bristol as they gallop away with the boy.

Hawkes and Montana rush to town for horses. Out of concern for his friend's safety, Hawkes refuses Montana's offer to help save his son. Montana, however, stealthily follows his friend, who eventually stops to camp for the night. As Hawkes gears up the next morning, a giant grizzly bear, played by Bart, explodes out of the pines. He charges into Hawkes' camp, and the chase is on — and it's a long one. Hawkes and Montana run like hell until they meet the edge of a cliff. Then, Butch-Cassidy-and-the-Sundance-Kid style, they do an "Oh shi-i-i-i-t" plunge into the river below. Bart, undeterred, slides down a steep slope to the riverbank.

"I know all about bears; they don't go near the water," says

Montana.

Wrong. Bart goes into the water after them, and the heroes run for their lives again. The scene with the heroes running from Bart was very real; no split screen. Doug ran even faster ahead of the actors, just out of frame. They stumble upon a dusty road where — by chance — a buckboard wagon with a team of horses is rumbling by. Hawkes and Montana manage a headfirst dive into the buckboard.

"Cut! That was terrific," shouted the director.

Bart the Bear catches the wagon carrying Kenny Rogers and crew on the set of *The Gambler: The Adventure Continues*.

Doug and the stunt coordinator, our friend Dave Cass, set up the next shot, calling for the buckboard to outrun the bear. Now, horses evolved alongside bears and are too smart to share a scene with a grizzly. The team of horses was replaced by a truck with a long trailer hitch. Dave asked Doug how fast the truck needed to go to outrun Bart — keeping him in the scene while leaving him in the dust. Doug estimated 15 miles per hour. I put Bart on his mark, and Doug positioned himself in the bed of the buckboard, behind Kenny and Bruce and alongside the camera.

The cameras rolled. Action! Doug called for Bart to run fast — and he did. He damn well caught the back of the buckboard with his massive forelegs, back legs spinning like a giant wind-up bear toy as he struggled to get a back foot onto the bed of the wagon. If the truck had slowed down, Bart would have been in the wagon bed atop stars. Doug told the driver to speed up. As the truck hit 25 miles per hour, Bart lost his grip and turned away with an "Oh shucks" stomp as the buckboard left the scene.

If you ever see the old western classic, the look of terror that Kenny and Bruce throw over their shoulders to the cameras was not acting, it was real terror. The scene of Bart half in the wagon was not scripted and could never have been — it was pure serendipity. It turned out to be a cinematic treasure.

Doug and I ran to our beautiful Bart and praised him with grapes, cookies, hugs, and back rubs, as Kenny and Bruce headed to the wardrobe trailer for a change of underwear.

~~~~~~~~~~~~~~~~~~~~~~~~

Clan of the Cave Bear

The next project would carry us to new heights. Jean M. Auel had written a bestseller called *Clan of the Cave Bear*. Warner Brothers had bought the screen rights. I (and about a million others) had read the novel, which is set some 40,000 years ago, as Cro-Magnons were displacing Neanderthals. A Cro-Magnon child orphaned by an earthquake is found and reluctantly taken in by a band of Neanderthals. She is tiny, delicate, and blond. Obviously one of "the Others," she is mistrusted and abused by some members of her new clan.

The film was directed by Michael Chapman, who was best known for *Taxi Driver* and *Raging Bull*. The cast featured Daryl Hannah, the disturbingly beautiful, uniquely talented actress from *Splash*. James Remar and Tommy Waits played the lead Neanderthals. The script called for a believable scene of a giant bear being stabbed to death by three naked, spear-wielding Neanderthals.

It was the '80s, when the filming of trained wild animals was still developing as an art. The 35-mm reels of film had to be hand-loaded into zippered black bags, shipped to Kodak, developed, printed, and rushed back for daily screenings, known as "dailies." From the dailies, the director and editor would form the rough cut. The bear was real, and the Neanderthals were played by real men; the only fakes were the spearheads that were made of rubber instead of chipped stone.

During our preparations for the film, our dear Daniels Creek neighbors got a real treat. We had to prep in full wardrobe and makeup. Our son Clint, now 22, had joined our team, and we had a good helper named John Malcolm. Bart knew these three as well as anyone, but he needed to get used to seeing them pretty much naked with wigs glued to rubber brow ridges. The guys' costumes were teeny leather thongs that could fit in the palm of your hand. The real challenges were the prosthetic brow ridges (think Neanderthal) and dark-brown, full-body makeup with red ocher ceremonial symbols. The black masks painted on their faces made their blue eyes stand out like marbles. The wigs were shoulder-length, black dreadlocks. We prepped in the open field across the street from our house. At the time, it was the only open space without livestock. We could explain to the neighbors what we were doing, but many passersby drove into the irrigation ditch at the side of the road. I mean, how often does one see three cavemen, naked butt cheeks and all, poking spears at a towering, raging bear? Bart was having terrific fun with the new game. I would imagine him thinking to himself, "Oh, my dear humans, what the hell will you think up next?"

Production sent me a long, blonde wig and a leather tunic that doubled Daryl Hannah's wardrobe for an over-the-shoulder shot with Bart. I made little caveman costumes for the kids. Jed was a mini-Doug in a black wig with body paint and a spear. Sausha already had long, blond hair, and I made her a little leather tunic like mine. We did a family portrait with Bart looming behind us. and sent it out as a Christmas card saying, "See what happens when you live with bears." Doug's mother hated it.

The movie was being filmed in Vancouver, British Columbia, and crossing the border had become a bit more complicated. Bart now had his own "passport" thanks to the U.S. and Canadian Convention on the International Trade of Endangered Species. Technically, a Canadian vet was required to do a health check so Bart could be properly "vetted" to enter Canada. As we pulled across the border, the vet stood at the ready — rectal thermometer in hand. When we opened the trailer door, he looked at Bart and then at the thermometer. Clearing his throat, he said authoritatively, "That is the healthiest bear I've ever seen," and signed the health certificate.

We arrived at a set that was built inside a massive warehouse. The art department had done a great job. The set looked Pleistocene in every detail. Doug had given the set builders specific instructions, and we thought everything was perfect ... until Bart

Bart the Bear, Doug in full costume, and the kids and I dressed as Neanderthals, while filming *Clan of the Cave Bear*.

Clint and Doug with Bart the Bear and other cast members in a scene from *Clan of the Cave Bear*.

walked into the cave. It was made of paper mache and coffee-cup-thick Styrofoam. All Bart had to do was sniff a wall and it crumbled. When it crumbled, it made a hole that was just big enough to put a claw in, which made a hole big enough to put his paw in, which made a hole big enough to put his head through. The director yelled, screamed, cried, "A-l-l-e-x!" The head of the art department came running. The next day, the cave was reinforced with quick-drying gunite.

In the script, the entire clan assembles before a cave in "the sacred ceremony of the cave bear." A great bear is baited from his lair by three young Neanderthal men determined to take on "the spirit of the bear" and establish their bravery and ability to lead. When one of the men is badly mauled, Ayla, the Cro-Magnon orphan, now a strong and confident "medicine woman," rushes unarmed to minister to the wounded warrior. The raging bear moves toward her, but she stands to face him down, imbued with the strong spirit of the cave lion. The bear turns away from her. To impress Ayla, one of the young men throws himself at the bear armed only with a knife and is decapitated. Doug then leaps onto Bart's back, sticking to him like a second skin, gripping with one hand and knees while repeatedly plunging the retractable rubber knife into Bart's neck. All the while, Clint and our other assistant trainer, John Malcom, jab Bart with spears. Bart could have kept it up for hours, but the action had to move along to the death scene. The cave bear lay down on his side, believably dead.

I was in costume and makeup as a stunt double, but Daryl Hannah decided to do her own scene with Bart. (It was a good thing, too.; Curvy and five feet, three inches tall, I was a better double for Dolly Parton than for the lovely, willowy, and long-legged Daryl Hannah.) She was terrific. The real-life, face-to-face confrontation on set was breathtaking and heart-pounding. The director walked to Doug, grabbed his hand, and said, "There is a new star in Hollywood!"

Daryl Hannah faces down with Bart the Bear as Doug provides instruction at her feet in *Clan of the Cave Bear*.

He wasn't talking about Doug.

Hauling Bart back from the Canadian coast to our home in the Rockies held a deeper meaning for us — we had made it out of the "canyon." Little did we know we were to spend the next three years of our lives making the most epic animal film of all time, and a chance encounter with a large rodent would set us on a lifelong mission.

The Bear

The Bear was adapted from James Oliver Curwood's *The Grizzly King,* published in 1916. The short novel is based on Curwood's unexpected emotional reaction to wantonly killing four grizzlies on a mountainside. In the preface, he states, "I destroyed possibly one hundred twenty years of life in twenty minutes. To kill not for meat but for the lust of slaughter amounts to murder. The greatest thrill is not to kill but to let live."

In the movie, two stories intertwine. Two men hunt for bears in Canada at the turn of the 19th century. That same summer, a six-month-old bear cub is orphaned when his mother dies in a landslide. The lost and lonely cub sees and follows a gigantic male bear who has been shot deep in his shoulder by the hunters. The injured, angry male has no use for the cub until, as he lies exhausted in a pool of mud, the cub comes to lick his wound clean. They bond. The cub is captured by the hunters. When one of the hunters goes for water without his rifle, he is trapped on the edge of the cliff by the giant bear. Instead of killing him, the bear lets him live. The event changes the man's life. The hunters release the cub back into the forest. The abandoned cub is about to be attacked by a cougar when his giant protector appears. Together, the "grizzly king" and his adopted cub climb through falling snow to their winter den.

The director, Jean-Jacques Annaud, had read Curwood's book as a boy in France. When he undertook the project, he was the most acclaimed and award-winning director in France and was fully

Bart the Bear and an unrelated cub share an iconic scene in *The Bear*.

aware of his success. He soared to fame with *Black and White in Color*, which won the Academy Award for Best Foreign Language Film in 1976. In 1982, *Quest for Fire* won him the César Awards (the French equivalent of an Oscar) for Best Film and Best Director. In 1987, *The Name of The Rose* won the César Award for Best Foreign Film. *The Bear* would win him the César Award for Best Director in 1988.

In 1981, after the success of *Quest for Fire*, a film that revolves around prehistoric man's taming of fire, Jean-Jacques and Gérard Brach began to collaborate on Curwood's novel. Both men shared a taste for the impossible. Their producer was Claude Berri. In 1982, they finished the synopsis for *The Bear*. The next summer, we received a visit from Jean-Jacques and one of Claude Berri's pillar producers, Pierre Grunstein. For six months, they searched all over Europe, Canada, and even Australia for a bear to play the epic role of Karr, the grizzly king. Most of the bears they met were pitiful. They had been declawed and defanged, and their personalities and power had been destroyed by the surgical processes. Most also had a lip-ring or were muzzled.

Their search ended in Utah. When they saw the six-year-old Bart, they stepped back. When they saw Bart and Doug together, they were speechless. When they saw Bart's behaviors, they beamed with joy. They had almost concluded that the film was impossible, but now they could proceed with preproduction. Jean-Jacques spent the rest of the day with the screenplay in hand, explaining Bart's character, Karr, and his vision for "the impossible film."

The French filmmakers had been told by bear biologists that it would be biologically impossible to have a cub work with an adult bear that was not its mother, and that a mature male would kill the cub immediately. For Jean-Jacques, the greater the challenge, the greater the achievement. He decided to mix real bears with animatronic bears or mimes in bear suits for the intimate scenes and close-ups. The Frenchmen returned to Paris to polish the script — all 400 pages and 1,007 scenes. Each scene was sketched into a storyboard, a series of drawings that illustrated in detail what Jean-Jacques wanted to see on the screen.

We began training. We bought dozens of stuffed teddy bears and asked Bart to give them "easy kisses" … we went through a lot of teddy bears. Finally, he chose to obey our wishes and ended up licking the stuffed toys as delicately as a two-year-old licks a lollipop. We trained him to limp, one huge foreleg held tightly against his chest, and to wear a prosthetic wound glued to his shoulder. He allowed us to dribble fake blood from the "gunshot hole" down his front paw. He learned to wallow, just so, in a pool of mud, to hold a fake fish in his mouth and take it to his teddy bear, and so much more.

As we trained, Jean-Jacques and Pierre traveled the globe in search of locations for the film. Curwood's novel takes place in British Columbia, Canada, an incredible province with intensely wild places, peaks that reach over 13,000 feet, and a surreal, autumnal light unique to Canada. But those locations were accessible only by helicopter. The producers shuddered at the thought. The team considered Alaska, the Spanish side of the Pyrenees, the Hungarian Carpathian Mountains, and even New Zealand. They also considered the Rockies of Utah — after all, that is where the star lived — but the French franc had fallen against the dollar, and anyway, the mountain wilderness areas of Utah were too small and crowded with cattle. The producers decided on the Dolomite Mountains of northern Italy.

In 1984, Jean-Jacques and Pierre returned to Utah. We spent four days poring over massive storyboards. The bear and the cub were in almost every scene. There would be just three human actors and only 16 words of dialogue in the entire film. Every scene would be filmed in vast, wild landscapes. There would never be another script or film like it, shot from the bears' point of view, taking the audience inside the bears' emotions, passions, and logic.

We trained for two years while Jean-Jacques and Claude Berri filmed Umberto Eco's *The Name of the Rose*, starring Sean Connery. By January 1987, we had a special trailer built for Bart that would fit inside a jumbo jet.

Then came a last-minute snag in the negotiations. Two years of training might all have been for naught. The contract provided tickets for Doug, me, and Clint, but would not pay one cent for our younger children — no tickets and no accommodations. It also didn't include return passage for Bart, an impossible expense for us at that time. We negotiated. We would

Sausha and Jed on location in Europe during the filming of *The Bear* in 1986. The production team considered them "excess baggage."

assume all expenses for our children. I did not care if we had to pay for their tickets and extra rooms, or even if I had to keep them with me in the cab of the truck while we were filming. There was no way on God's green earth I would leave them for six months. I also knew there was no way Doug and Clint could do it without me. They knew it, too. But we would not budge on the matter of Bart's return ticket. With all the permits, trucks, jumbo jets, and more, his return trip would cost around $40,000 (big bucks back in those days). For three days, we held our ground (and our breath). Finally, on day four, FedEx delivered the signed agreement with Bart's return ticket prepaid and guaranteed.

And then began the adventure. We flew out of Los Angeles because that was the closest airport big enough for a 747. Our direct flight from Los Angeles to Frankfurt, Germany was on a huge Lufthansa jumbo jet that was half cargo and half passenger cabin. I'm quite sure the pilot did not come on the intercom to announce just what and who was in the cargo deck below. We left the truck in storage at the Los Angeles airport. On the tarmac, a giant scissor-lift hoisted Bart and his trailer, all 8,000 pounds, into the cargo hold. As I watched, I had to remind myself that they fly army tanks all over the world. Doug and Clint were given portable oxygen masks, pillows, and blankets so they could stay alongside Bart in the cargo hold. The children and I were on another flight that would arrive in Frankfurt several hours earlier.

3,000 pounds of bear and trailer being loaded into the plane that will carry them from Los Angeles to Frankfurt.

The production company totally forgot about my kids and me.

We ended up on a luggage cart for 16 hours. It was long before the days of cell phones. I found the currency exchange booth and a pay phone and called the only number I had for the production office in Paris, but no one there spoke English. I pushed Jed and Sausha around in the cart, finally finding a German who could speak French and English to help me try to phone production. The office was closed.

Doug was busy getting our 1,500-pound bear off the tarmac and through customs in Frankfurt. It was not until he got to the hotel that he asked, "Hey, has anyone seen my wife and kids?" Finally, a multilingual German production assistant raced to the airport to find the three of us draped like wet socks over the luggage cart.

Reunited with Doug, Clint, Bart, and somewhat rested, we climbed into the German Pinzgauer truck and began to pull Bart and his trailer down the Autobahn to Northern Italy. At that time, there was absolutely no speed limit on the Autobahn. It was early May, and Bart was shedding. As we rocketed along the German Indianapolis 500, bits and tufts of Bart's fur flew like golden dragonflies from the trailer vents. I wondered if there ever had been bits of Kodiak fur and fluff bouncing off windshields on the Autobahn … probably not.

We arrived in San Virgilio, Italy. The town still had medieval walls and gates. I had always dreamed of seeing medieval Europe and wanted to float through my crown chakra and time travel, but I had to stay grounded; there were a lot of pieces to hold together. A couple of those pieces were a seven-year-old and a ten-year-old who were considered so much extra baggage by production. Then, a small miracle happened. A production manager's fiancé was looking for employment on the movie. She was 20, beautiful, smart, sweet, and spoke six languages. It seemed to me that Julie Andrews had just stepped out of *The Sound of Music*. I caught my breath and asked her if she would consider being our nanny. Production would most likely let her bunk with her fiancé, and I would pay all her expenses and a good wage. She was the answer to a prayer. Her name was Stephanie. Jed and Sausha adored her. We still do.

Then, it truly began. The producers had, somehow, sourced every bear cub in Eastern and Western Europe and the United Kingdom from zoos, circuses, and game farms. They were all European brown bears — smaller than the North American brown bear and with slightly larger ears. The cubs numbered 17 in all. The crew came from all over Europe. I believe there were over ten nationalities represented. Every day, there were four call sheets in French, German, English, and Italian.

Our family were just about the only Americans. I had my first experience with bigotry. I had no idea that people from America had no culture, nuance, sophistication, or palate, and that Americans could not appreciate the difference between two-star and five-star hotels. If you were not French ... well, you were not French. Looking back, I see it was a good lesson in compassion for me to experience what it feels like to be looked down upon. We learned another lesson from the French that was easier to swallow. In Utah, if you only had $10 for dinner, you spent it on a burger, fries, and a shake. In France, $10 would be spent on bread and cheese, wine, and flowers.

Puppeteers and control cables for the animatronic cub that was never used in *The Bear*.

Food for the belly, wine for the spirit, and flowers for the soul — not a bad idea.

From the beginning, the plan was that every time the actual big bear and cub were to be in the same scene, either the cub would be animatronic or the big bear would be a mime in a bear suit. Production had hired the best in the world of animatronics, Jim Henson's Creature Shop out of London. And thank God for them. More than once, their Monty Python sense of humor saved us from taking ourselves too seriously. However, as good as the animatronics were — truly the best in the world — it just wasn't working. The real bears made the animatronics look like what they were: puppets, fake, lifeless. Jean-Jacques was a master in the art of filmmaking, but even his genius could not make the fake bears look real. Doug was a master in understanding the mind of the grizzly; perhaps he could do the impossible.

Early in production, we were shooting a scene with Bart and the animatronic cub. Eight sets of wires led to eight puppeteers, two

Prepping for what many believed was impossible — Doug with Bart the Bear and an unrelated cub, who would share scenes in *The Bear*.

just for the tongue. The Henson team worked their hearts out making new models — different fur, more wires, more puppeteers — but it seems that only God can make a bear.

Doug asked Pierre Grunstein to take a moment with us. "Pierre, this is nonsense. This film can be a masterpiece or a Muppet Show. Let us try. Give us our choice of two cubs and two weeks. Let us try." The producer was thrown off balance. He and Jean-Jacques had spent five years in preproduction, meticulously storyboarding every scene with the real bears and the puppets. They had already spent over a million dollars on the animatronics and the puppeteers. But it would be an unimaginable first — a mature male bear working beside an unrelated cub.

The director, producers, and French veterinarians agreed

Doug holds an animatronic bear head while prepping for *The Bear*.

that it was impossible ... but if anyone could do it, it would be the Seus family.

Here is how we did it. From the pod of cubs, we chose four-month-old siblings that belonged to a German trainer. We named them Ben and Bonnie. We introduced the bedding hay from the cubs' pens to Bart and gave Bart's bedding to the cubs. They smelled each other for days before they met. Then they saw each other from 50 yards, then 40, 30, 20, 10. Bart had long been trained to stay on his mark. The cubs soon learned that when they stayed on a 12" x 12" wooden board, a cookie would just pop into their mouths.

Bart tolerated the little male cub, Ben, but seemed to prefer the petite female, Bonnie. Even though it would be three years before she would be reproductively receptive, Bart seemed to know she might be pretty interesting one day. I believe Bart understood that accepting these cubs not of his loins conflicted with his natural instincts. But I also believe he understood our desperation in asking him to overcome inner bearness and do it for us.

Jean-Jacques had been on another location filming the actors. By the time he came to see us, we had Bart and Bonnie within three feet of each other, crawling on their bellies, prepared for a scene where they sneak up on a stag. Always in utter control of himself, completely composed, hands behind his back, Jean-Jacques melted. He had tears in his eyes when he said, "This is fantastic; this is spectacular. Now I have my story."

It happened to be the wettest and coldest summer in Northern Italy for years. The sky was always touching the ground. It rained endlessly. Scene by scene, we climbed higher and higher into the Dolomites … Misurnia, Logo de Calaila, Prado, Fiera di Primiero, and finally, a tiny village called Zortia, as high as one could go by car. Beyond that, there were just hiking trails. We walked. Bart's trailer was moved by a Unimog, a small, army-tank-like contraption. We had reached a majestic setting of jagged white peaks — mountains so high that one strained to see their tops.

Then came a moment that had absolutely nothing to do with the film but would change the course of our lives.

One morning, the art director, Uri, and I were stuffing strawberry jam into sausage casings to serve as entrails in the taxidermic stag that Karr had killed. The scene called for Karr and the cub to feast together on the carcass. Suddenly, there was a commotion on the next rise. The crew and a few alpine hikers were gathered around some sort of wondrous sight. We rushed to see what the spectacle might be. There, sitting on a stone outcropping, was a golden Marmot. "Oh, for Pete's sake, Uri," I laughed, "that is just a rock chuck!" He looked back at me and said seriously, "You don't understand, Lynne; that is all we have left." I quit laughing.

That night, I sat alone with Bart and realized his life in our human world had to matter for something more than movies … something much more. I wasn't sure how or when or where we could help, but our Rocky Mountains were still wildly alive and must not become the dead, silent landscape of the Dolomites.

It would be impossible to share every story from the making of The Bear. We worked 16-hour days, seven days a week, without holidays

Bart the Bear and an orphaned cub share an elk carcass while filming The Bear. It was the ultimate test of what many believed was an impossible relationship.

or breaks. Sometimes we would leave one location to be in another town on call the next day, having driven most of the night. It was Europe. There were no union rules, no humane society representative on set. So many stories — triumphs and tenderness, jubilant ecstasy, despondency, depression, blissful brilliance. So many stories.

Jean-Jacques and Doug were both 43 years old and at a stage in a man's career when he must achieve greatness... or not. There is a book called The Rat Within. The rat is the ego that gnaws at a man's soul — a powerfully determined rat will gnaw through most anything or anyone to get to the prize; it lies within the best, the bravest, and the most brilliant of them all. Both men knew the rat intimately. Jean-Jacques' was hidden and cunningly treacherous. Doug wore his on his sleeve, capricious and ready to strike. Bart was as on edge and raw-nerved as Doug was. They bounced around each other like electrons in an atom, but the nucleus of love and trust between them could not be split.

I tried to understand the male ego, but I did not like the rat one bit. If the rat didn't leave when we got home, I would.

We were supposed to have wrapped by the end of August, and indeed, the other trainers and over half the crew were sent home by then. Our time was extended until the end of September. Our last location was Lienz, Austria, which looked just like a postcard with red geraniums trailing from the window boxes of wooden Alpine houses. The women wore dirndl dresses; the men often wore lederhosen and Tyrolean hats. The knee-deep wildflower fields were graced with gentle golden cows whose huge brass bells chimed from their necks. The 13th-century Burg Bruck castle towered over the town. At least we had an enchanting setting to strain ourselves to the sinew-splitting limit.

Fortunately, on the flight home, the rat bailed somewhere over the Atlantic. The time of lilacs would come again.

Doug prepping Bart the Bear for a formidable strike in *The Bear*.

The Glory Years

The next 12 years of our life with Bart were headlong and full tilt — a bobsled run. He was in his prime, and so were we. There were starts, stops, dangerous curves, speed bumps, and finish lines. Bart was the machine, Doug was the driver, and I was the brake woman.

Fortunately, the first movie we did after *The Bear* was a comedy, *The Great Outdoors*, with John Candy and Dan Aykroyd. While we were still unpacking from Europe, the phone rang. "Hello, this is Universal Studios. We have a script that needs a humongous bear with a shaved head and then a shaved butt." I wondered which one of our friends was welcoming us home with this demented joke, but the call was for real, and soon we were making notes on the screenplay. The big bear's bald patches were the result of being blasted by a shotgun. Of course, we were not about to shave the top of Bart's head, never mind his butt. However, we would consider a prosthetic bald cap and a rubber butt piece. After all, Bart had let us glue a "gunshot wound" on his shoulder for several months during *The Bear*.

If it were filmed today, all the bald parts would be created in post-production with computer-generated images, but in 1988, everything was the magic of the art department. The bald head and butt prosthetics were made by the famous visual effects team that had just finished *Robocop*. The headpieces were expensive and time-consuming to produce. For training, we used a baseball hat instead.

Bart thought it was one of his easiest jobs ever, "Just wear this stupid hat, and I will get a lot of grapes."

We secured the bald prosthetic to Bart's head with surgical adhesive. That wasn't a problem until the end of the day when the producer asked us to please remove the piece for the next day's shoot. "They are very expensive," he said. Well, have you ever pulled a big adhesive bandage from a hairy place on your body? Our reply to the producer was, "If you really want it, you take it off." So, we would load Bart, headpiece and all, for the night, and every night he would carefully pick the damn thing off his head and tear it into little pieces. (I saved the pieces and glued them to the heads of teddy bears that I sent to the crew as Christmas presents.)

We filmed right at Universal Studios on one of their largest sound stages. Bart spent the nights in his trailer parked behind the old *Psycho* set. The spooky old Victorian house still loomed behind the Bates Motel. The shoot was a merry-go-round of laughs. An extraordinary treat was John Candy himself. Between the scenes, instead of retreating to his trailer, he would stand by the craft service table eating maple-frosted doughnuts and entertaining the crew with running stand-up comedy. The man was a gem.

One of the most memorable bear stunts of all time was bald-headed Bart, a legendary man-eating bear, chasing John Candy through the woods — filmed at night in the pouring rain. John barely makes it inside the cabin, holds the door closed with his arms

In a scene from *The Great Outdoors*, Bart the Bear crushes Clint, John Candy's double, under a door.

wide, saying breathlessly, "Big bear ... big bear ... chase me," and then, WHAM! Bart crashes down the door, crushing John under it, then bounces repeatedly on the door like a kid on an inner tube. Bart marches into the cabin, terrorizing two screaming families. Dan Aykroyd tries to chase Bart off with a fireplace implement that is swatted away, retreats upstairs to protect his family, and is trying to fend off Bart by jamming a canoe oar in his jaws when a neighbor arrives with a gun — an ancient, double-barreled shotgun that had been converted into a floor lamp but is somehow loaded and still functions. Candy grabs the gun away from the neighbor, takes aim at Bart's butt, and creates the second bald patch. Bart, displaying amazingly human-like bare buttocks, makes a hasty retreat, moaning and bellowing into the night.

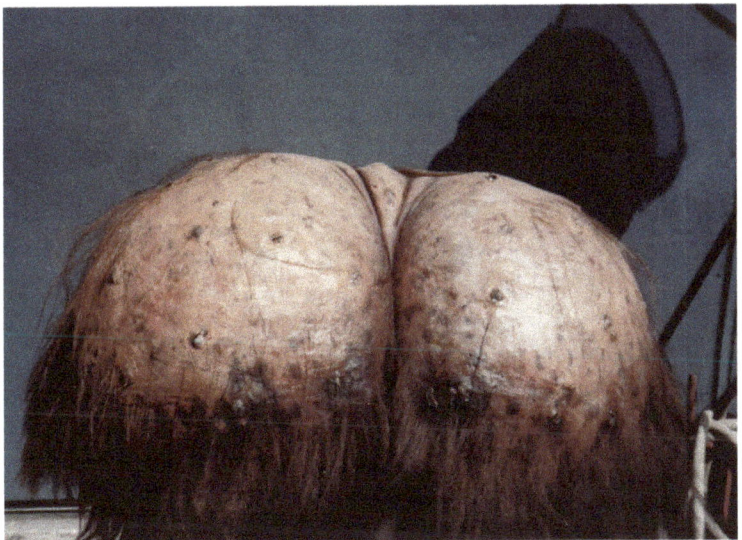

The prosthetic butt piece that Bart the Bear wore in *The Great Outdoors*.

Despite his complaints that it cost "half a Honda" to replace Bart's headpiece every day, we became very fond of the producer, Arne Schmidt. One day on set, Arne, who was enamored of Bart, asked us what environmental group did the most for bear conservation. Thinking it over, we realized there really wasn't one that focused on grizzly bears and the critical habitat needed to connect the dwindling, isolated, and genetically endangered populations. I remembered the lonely marmot in the wildlife-deprived mountains of the old world.

Well, maybe we should, maybe we could ... at that moment, The Vital Ground Foundation was conceived. Arne reached out to some of his conservation-minded Hollywood friends, and we reached out to our hiking-boot bear-loving buddies, Doug Peacock and Doug Chadwick.

Chadwick had appeared at our door one winter's eve in 1984. He was writing a *National Geographic* article, "GRIZZ — Of Man and the Great Bear." In the story, a full-page photo of Doug sitting casually on Bart's back bespoke the friendship possible between a human and *horribilis*. Chadwick wrote of the desperate decline of the grizzly bear in the lower 48 states. His words at the end spoke to our souls: "Where our last frontiers remain good enough for the grizzly, they will be good enough for all the other wild things that need homes and a little respect. And they will be good enough, big enough, wild enough, free enough for us." There was also a very special woman in our lives who understood these words. Susan Bridges became a founding Vital Ground board member and served as our first Board Secretary. She was an integral part of the foundation.

Doug and I with The Vital Ground Foundation's first deed for property we purchased after draining our retirement account.

Bog Kesling

We cashed in our second attempt at a retirement account and bought 240 acres on the Teton River, prime grizzly bear and wildlife habitat on the Rocky Mountain Front in Montana. The name on the deed was Vital Ground! Bart's legacy began with that prime patch of wildland that would be protected forever. Vital Ground was an official 501(c)(3), complete with a board of directors. Arne Schmidt was the first Chairman of the Board.

The next stop was the charming, Bavarian-style town of Leavenworth in the Cascade Mountains of central Washington State. The nearby Wenatchee River was the location for *On Deadly Ground*, a Warner Brothers action/adventure/thriller directed by and starring Steven Seagal. It was pure Seagal: balls out, big guns, massive explosions, black-belt karate fights, and lots more guns. Nevertheless, the plot was just our cup of tea. The evil Aegis Oil Company and their demon CEO, played by Michael Caine, were raping the land and the lifeways of the Eskimo people. Enter the environmental warrior, Seagal, who battles the big oil money bad guys and saves a beautiful native woman from a very big bear with just a little bitty knife. For all the nonsense, the speech Seagal gives at the end of the film is pure conservation gold. At the premiere of *On Deadly Ground*, Mr. Seagal saw to it that Warner Brothers

Bart the Bear laughing at Doug dressed as Steven Seagal for *On Deadly Ground*.

donated the proceeds from the premier to Vital Ground — thirty thousand dollars for wild things and their wild places. Maybe we *could* do this.

~~~~~~~~~~~~~~~~~~~~~~~~

Stay Tuned

Warner Brothers' film *Stay Tuned* in 1992 was perhaps the most imaginative script we have ever received. John Ritter and Pam Dawber somehow manage to get sucked into a fuzzy television screen. Then, TV show by TV show, they fall into whacky, crazy, and sometimes hellish adventures. Lucky for us, they also get trapped in a

Doug training Raven to jump from the shed for *Stay Tuned*.

Doug fending off a wolf attack with a fiery prop stick in *Stay Tuned*.

shot-in-the-wild nature show. We shot in Whistler, Canada, with our buddy, Arne Schmidt who was the line producer. Like us, he brought his family, which included a son and a daughter close in age to Jed and Sausha. All the time we were filming, our kids were having a ball skiing the slopes of Whistler Mountain.

The bizarre family movie has one of the best wolf scenes we have ever put in a film. The stars are pursued by a pack of wolves and seek refuge on a frozen lakebed, where they shelter in an ice shack. The wolves beat down the door and try to attack the terrified humans across a fire they had built to keep themselves from freezing. Raven, one of our blackest wolves, snarls across the fire. John Ritter takes a red-embered limb from the fire and fends them off. Of course, it was Doug, Clint, and me in heavy parkas eliciting the behaviors with chunks of corned beef. The captives escape by chopping a hole through the ice, through which they fall into a cartoon movie and turn into mice.

It was a comedy, but the wolf work was as demanding as *White Fang*, the movie we would do the following year. We trained wolves for the attacks by encouraging them to jump on us for a chunk of raw meat in our hands. The hard part was teaching them the difference between the meat and a human hand full of tiny bones. We had kept the wolves hungry for the film, and they were brilliant. Each was rewarded with a whole prime rib. We said goodbye to Arne and his family, who would become forever friends, and headed home.

~~~~~~~~~~~~~~~~~~~~~~~~

White Fang

The next touchdown was a long one in Haines, Alaska. Disney was remaking Jack London's *White Fang*, starring a beardless young Ethan Hawke and an aging Klaus Maria Brandauer. The classic story was chock-full of dogs, wolf-dogs, wild wolf packs, and one great big bear. Our Clint landed a nice part in the film as Tinker, the "dumb" bad guy. Clint's dog, Junior, had a significant role in the movie as well. Wonderful! It was time for Clint to follow his own star, although that left just Doug and me to wrangle eight wolves and Bart. Jed and Sausha, at 10 and 13, didn't need a nanny but were too young to be assistant animal trainers. We were shorthanded, to say the least.

The previous summer, we were on a family camping trip when we lost a wheel bearing at Pahaska Tepee Resort in Yellowstone National Park. A lanky fellow helped us turn a Coke can into a hub cover. He mentioned that he knew all the local bears in Wyoming's Absaroka Mountains by their number. His favorite was #104. (Bear biologists give study bears numbers instead of names. It is an academic and scientific practice so that one does not become emotionally attached to them.)

His name was Scott Smith, but everyone called him Smitty. Upon parting, he said, "If you guys ever are looking for help …" He would join us in Alaska to film *White Fang*, and for the three decades since, he has been our right-hand man — serendipity in a wheel bearing.

Bart the Bear in hot pursuit of Ethan Hawke in *White Fang*.

Randal Keizer, the director, was kind, and the enthusiasm of teenaged Ethan Hawke as Jack Connell was delightfully endearing. The golden moment of the film has Jack meandering through the countryside, admiring the wildlife, when Bart suddenly looms behind him (a freeze frame of the shot became a poster for the film), and the chase is on. Jack survives by diving headfirst into a cranny in an enormous beaver den. From inside the pile of logs, the director and the camera crew watched. Bart's huge claws ripped the den apart, making a hole big enough for his giant head to loom through — fangs bared, paw clawing at Ethan's legs, and drool hitting the camera lens. The look on their faces was indescribable!

Even though Bart is the star of our story, the wolves were

brilliant costars. Oh, the wolves, moving like a flock of birds flying low over the tundra. Their freeze-proof, snowshoe paws flashing through mists of crystals in the freezing air, ears back, tongues lolling, jaws smiling wide, and fire eyes flashing! Teton, Peach, Koda, Yukon, Moon, Booboo, Shadow, and Silver. I still found myself burying my face in their ruffs to smell the scent of sweet, fresh-cut hay like when they were pups. Exquisite wolves!

One of our main locations was an open valley called Porcupine Creek, an hour from Haines. That February, the temperature was seldom above zero. The mountains were fierce and formidable — not one road scarred their deep, white, secluded places. One would have to hike and climb to penetrate them. But they seemed to

Our exquisite pack of wolves c. 1990.

whisper, "Do not disrespect me; I can kill you."

We filmed for weeks on the frozen tundra. I got frostbite on the fourth toe of my left foot; to this day, it has no color. The first assistant director ordered me Army-issue arctic gear, so-called "Mickey Mouse boots" because that is what the black, bulbous footwear resembled. The heavy rubber boots did not come in women's size six, but with four pairs of thick wool socks, they fit fine and did the trick. I looked like I had clown feet. The wolves thought the boots were rubber fetch toys. We had to settle that.

Bart and the wolves were kept in a shelter out on the Porcupine Creek location to save them from the daily drive. We were transported by car. Our driver was a Tlingit woman named Emma. For whatever reason, Doug and I have always been drawn to Native American cultures and nature-based belief systems. Perhaps because as we understand it, Animism, the belief that the earth, nature, and everything in it is alive with the power of the Divine Mystery, needs no doctrine to be perceived. There is also not much church attendance required, and all the scripture one needs is written deep inside a tree. We were elated to find a name for what we believed in our hearts to be true.

I'm sure we were driving Emma nuts with our endless questions about her culture. "How did the Russian and European invasions change the spiritual values and lifeways of your people? The early missionaries destroyed your totem poles as graven images, right? And they took away your button blankets? All the clans and families follow the maternal line and take the names of animals, right? And a member of the Raven Clan cannot marry a member of the Raven Clan, right? Which is your Clan? And how about the Chilkat blankets, muskox sheddings, and cedar bark? Does anyone still make them? And what about the Shaman journey and the wild creatures that present their tongues to them?"

That did it. She said, "Okay, okay, okay, I will take you to my grandfather."

Takakastina was a Tlingit elder. George Lewis was his Christian name. He had pewter hair, jet-black eyes, and skin whiter than mine. We sat at his knees like children. I think they indulged us because we "talked to bears and wolves." But the deep spiritual food we were asking for could only be given to relatives. To be adopted required a special potlatch ceremony where we would be given the names and take the places of departed family members. Being married, Doug and I could not be of the same moiety. The Eagles would pay the Ravens to adopt the burly, bearded grizzly man. The Ravens would pay the Eagles to take in the white wolf woman. We were told to fast for two days before the ceremony.

When the clans gathered, there was sweet cedar smoke, drumming, soft chanting, and praying. We were given special knowledge I cannot share. Then, with the laying on of hands, we were solemnly given our new names and family places. I became George's mother Takla-uea; Doug became George's brother, Kagontan. We were also given our TuKingjecks, our individual guardian spirits, and reminded that these guardians would leave a person who did evil or was immoral. George put Tlingit silver cuff bracelets on our wrists. He had carved the images himself. Mine was two wolves in profile. Doug's, of course, was a full-face bear. Our "adoption papers" were finely, fully beaded amulets to be worn over one's heart: a raven for Doug and an eagle for me. After the ceremony, we were called grandmother and uncle and kissed by our new relatives. Seated in our places of honor, the potlatch feast commenced with halibut cheeks, salmon in eulachon oil, roasted caribou with thimbleberry jam, coffee, and Black Velvet pipe tobacco.

We finished filming and left for home in June of that year. Raw, tender pieces of our hearts stayed with our Tlingit family. We kept in close touch with the family and George Lewis until his death in 1998. We left behind another part of our family on Porcupine Creek. Teton, our biggest and oldest wolf at 12, just left in his sleep one night. It had been such a joy to see him moving over the tundra with his pack. It was both sad and beautiful to bury him where he had been so free and happy the day before.

~~~~~~~~~~~~~~~~~~~~~~~

Tank and the New Pack

All our wolf kids were now seniors. We had raised that pack of wolves together from pups. Growing up with each other, they sort things out between themselves and select their leader. It was time to retire the Lobo veterans, who just preferred to lie in the shade of the creek in the summer and curl up in their dens of grass hay in the winter. I was ready for new pups. I love wolf pups. Domed heads the size of tennis balls, ears so tiny that they are hard to see in the spiky, shiny fur, tails as straight and slim as breadsticks, cat-claw toenails, and deep blue eyes already flashing fire. And, of course, that sweet, wild smell of new-cut hay. We sourced preserves and zoos that could sell to us with our USDA license. Our new pack included two arctic wolves, as white as ermines in the winter, Old Man and Cree; three blacks, Shadow, Ranger, and Raven; and two grays, Koda, and Yukon (we were recycling names).

We had a new dream for our new pack. The year Vital Ground received its official 501(c)(3) status, we were fortunate to be introduced to John and Frank Craighead. The twin brothers, who led the first grizzly protection efforts in the 1950s, are considered the fathers of grizzly bear conservation. But then came the real treasure — Jean Craighead George was the most brilliant, powerful woman I have ever known. She loved wolves. She wrote over 100 books, including *My Side of the Mountain*. Her masterpiece, Newberry Medal-winning *Julie of the Wolves*, is a literary legend.

Over the years, several screenplays were written for the latter, and some came close, so close, to being made. We always stood at the ready with "Julie's wolf pack." While the screenplay never came to fruition, John and Jean were deep supporters of Vital Ground and served on the advisory board for years. The Craighead name bestowed credibility on our fledgling organization.

The first Vital Ground gathering in Montana was in the spring of 1990 at the Pine Butte Nature Preserve, a stone's throw from the 240 acres we had first locked away into wildness. We trailered Bart, loaded our human kids and four wolf cubs, and headed north to Bob Scriver's ranch near Pine Butte. Jean was in attendance. She held my 13-year-old daughter as tenderly and tightly as she did wolf pups on her lap. We shared the blood of naturalists, and it made us family. Jean was a force of nature with her blue eyes, snow-white hair, booming voice, and hands as strong as any man's.

We had Jean in our life, like a precious jewel, until her death in 2012. She was my teacher, my mentor, and my icon. I loved her. I always will.

We were ready to add another member to our family. We needed a bear cub fix. After all, how long can one go without the T-Rex screams, mounds of poop, bandaged hands, and the smell of raw pumpkins?

There is a list of surplus zoo animals available to USDA-licensed, regularly inspected facilities such as ours. The list included exotic animals: zebras, flamingos,

My mentor, Jean Craighead George, with our baby wolf Koda.

water buffaloes, kangaroos, and large predators. We kept a close eye on the list, and in January, there he was, a brown bear who came close to spending his life behind bars.

We named him Tank because he would never walk around anything in his way; instead, he would just crawl up and over obstacles like an Army tank.

We had recently built an addition to our little 1919 farmhouse and designed a walk-in basement with tile floors and wainscoting. The floor had a drain like a shower. Voila, a perfect room for bringing up bears, wolves, cougars, and such in our family home! When Tank learned how to push open the door to the upstairs kitchen to see what I was making for dinner, I knew he was ready for an outdoor pen. It was almost May, and the air was once again lavender with lilacs and plum blossoms.

Our two-legged kids were teenagers. Sausha was junior class president, and her life was proms and parties. Jed was on the state champion wrestling team and was much more interested in pretty girls than bears or wolves. Between the two of them, we replaced fenders and tailgates on a regular basis. Life was good. Bart watched it all with the fondness of a loving uncle.

The bobsled was about to turn into a rocket ship.

Six-week-old Tank; no animal is more adorable than a bear cub.

A man in the arms of a massive grizzly, the man's head disappearing between the cavernous jaws of the bear like a candied apple. This image appears on movie screens, on television, online, and as a centerfold of National Geographic.

Joel Sartore

Rocket Ride

Jim Harrison was an American literary icon, sometimes compared to Hemingway and Steinbeck. His novella, *Legends of the Fall*, set in the wilds of Montana at the turn of the 19th century, spans half a century. His characters were brought to life by the masterful director Edward Zwick. Ed had a cast of pure gold to sculpt with: Anthony Hopkins, Brad Pitt, Aidan Quinn, Henry Thomas, Julia Ormond, Gordon Tootoosis, and Tantoo Cardinal. The passionate, hauntingly beautiful story of love, the horror of war, and the bonds of blood was undoubtedly the finest film we have ever been part of.

Brad Pitt's character, Tristan, played as a teenager by Eric Johnson, attempts a coup against a sleeping grizzly. The bear rages after him, and the two face off around the pillar of a tree. The "dance" ends with Tristan slashed by the bear's claws, and the boy's knife deep in the bear's paw, severing it. From then on, the boy has "the voice of the bear inside him." There is a scene in the middle of the film where One Stab, played by Gordon Tootoosis, tells the father and the brothers that he has spotted the old bear in a nearby meadow. Tristan, now a grown man, rushes to the cliff above the bear and takes aim, but he locks eyes with the bear and cannot pull the trigger. In a voice-over, One Stab explains Tristan's inability to kill the bear, "When a human and animal exchange blood, they become one spirit."

Tristan lives through heartbreaking tragedies to become an old man. The film's final scene, the mauling of Tristan by the bear, played by Doug and Bart, is legendary. The moment that Tristan and the bear die together is as poignant and piercing as the screech of the hawk and the cry of the Native flute that played in the background. The breathtaking cinematography of Legends of the Fall won the director of photography, John Toll, an Academy Award. It remains a mystery to me why Brad Pitt did not run away with the Oscar for best actor. If you are ever in the mood for a visceral drama that showcases the epitome of raw talent and exceptional filmmaking, watch or rewatch this masterpiece.

Brad had come in a few days early to spend time with the grizzly. As we chatted, he asked about the plight of the great bears in the wild. We told him about the fledgling efforts of Vital Ground. He said, "If there is ever anything I can do to help, let me know." But Brad would prove to be a man of his word, truly.

We filmed in the Canadian Rockies, just outside Banff National

Doug doubles as Brad Pitt in the final scene of Legends of the Fall.

Park. We stayed at the Nakoda Lodge, owned and operated by the Stoney Band of the Great Sioux Nation. The lodge was designed with high, vaulted ceilings to resemble tipis circled around a turquoise lake. It was the most tranquil place we have ever stayed while filming. The Stoney Sioux we met, with their chiseled cheeks the color of amber honey, were proudly gentle. We had breakfast every morning at the lodge and joked over coffee. "Say, aren't you Irish?" we would ask. "Sure are," they would reply, "And by the way, aren't you an Eskimo?"

Production had arranged a secure spot for Bart not far from our room, deep in the pines. One morning, as we were exercising Bart, we spotted a native elder standing as still as a tree, just barely in view. We met his eyes and nodded for him to come closer. Then we saw her. Behind him was a prepubescent girl, shy as a wounded sparrow. Her braids glinted in the dappled sunlight, shiny and black as oil. The old man soundlessly stepped closer. "Girl sick." He used his hands to sign crawling crabs to show that it was cancer. "We pray to Grandfather?" he asked, looking at Bart. We stepped aside, and he brought her forward. The high-pitched, minor tones of a Sioux prayer song resounded through the forest as he dusted Bart and the child with tobacco. To our astonishment, Bart sat as quietly as if he were attending a high holy mass. Native hands, as brown and worn as saddle leather, cupped around a match and a braid of sweet grass. Bart lifted his head to whiff the clove and lavender-scented smoke. The ancient Elder passed an eagle feather over us. Then, without a word, they slipped back into the forest like deer.

~~~~~~~~~~~~~~~~~~~~~~~~~~~

The Edge

While *Legends of the Fall* was the finest film we were ever part of, *The Edge* is considered by many to be our most outstanding work. As I see it, nothing involving a movie camera and a bear could ever surpass *The Bear*. Yet, *The Edge* seems paramount in people's minds as the capstone of Bart's career. The action/adventure/survival thriller took us back to the Bow River in the Canadian Rockies only two short years after we filmed *Legends of the Fall* there. The director was Lee Thomahori, an intense native New Zealander who had come to fame with *Once Were Warriors*. The screenwriter was David Mamet, a Pulitzer Prize winner known for "Mamet Speak." I didn't realize how famous he was until it took me an hour to read about him and his papers on Wikipedia. The cast was very small but mighty and included the incomparable Anthony Hopkins. We'd had the privilege of working with Anthony on *Legends of the Fall*, but he and Bart had never shared a scene. *The Edge* would put them nose-to-nose.

The plot is one of survival and deceit. A plane crashes in the wilderness, and the pilot is killed. A billionaire with an encyclopedic brain, played by Anthony, a photographer, played by Alec Baldwin, and his assistant, played by Harold Perrineau, begin the survival trial. Throw in a little intrigue — the billionaire's supermodel trophy wife, played by Elle McPherson, is having an affair with the photographer, who would love the wealthy husband dead and the gorgeous, rich widow all to himself.

Enter the monstrous, man-eating bear, and the fun begins. Early on, the bear attacks the trio at a nighttime campfire in pouring rain. The assistant is picked up by his thigh, shaken "to death," and dragged off into the darkness for dinner. That stunt goes down in the annals of American stunt work. We prepped for months, mainly because Harold Perrineau is an African American with dreadlocks. In the Screen Actors Guild Union, it is unacceptable for a white person to double a person of color. However, there was no Black stunt person willing to attempt the mauling scene with our grizzly bear. As Harold's stunt double, Doug had to train Bart while wearing a wig and full face and body makeup. Using a strap-on fiberglass mold of Doug's leg, he taught Bart to pick him up by it, shake him, and drag him into the woods.

The stormy scene was shot at night, with a wind machine, a

Bart the Bear and Doug prep for their big scene in *The Edge*.

The on-screen result of their preparation in *The Edge*.

rain machine that made rain as heavy as any shower head, and a blazing fire. I'm still not sure how the fire kept going with all that rain — it was movie magic. We were also highly aware that it was a full moon., and that moon pulls the same on man and bear. Doug took his place by the fire and called Bart from his mark — the scene is terrifying, jolting, beyond horrifying. The editors had to cut it down, or it would've been too gruesome for the screen. The result was Doug Seus and Bart the Bear's finest on-screen moment.

Most of the time, Clint doubled Alec, and Doug doubled Anthony — but Doug would always play whoever was closest to the bear. However, in a climactic scene with Anthony and Bart on a log over the river … it was actually Anthony and Bart. Lying low between them, touching Anthony's knee and Bart's paw, was Doug. That was it — no hotwires. Anthony had complete trust in Doug and his relationship with the immense, nine-foot-tall grizzly.

We were fortunate to share long conversations with Anthony, a true gentleman who graciously made time for everyone. He considered Bart his fellow thespian in every sense of the word. He had witnessed Bart acting — yes,

Clint as Anthony Hopkins and Doug as Alec Baldwin in *The Edge*.

acting; lowering his head, pinning back his ears, stiffening his lower lip, and digging his back claws deeper into the earth. It wasn't a result of training; his tenacity and energy came from within. Bart knew when he was on, and Anthony Hopkins, considered by many to be the world's greatest screen actor, knew it too.

A little side story here — Bart's favorite "paycheck" that summer was fresh pears. Throughout filming, Alec's shirt was heavy brown corduroy with two front pockets. The director of photography, Don McAlpine, thought it was just the funniest thing to hop off his camera seat and run over to put a juicy pear in each of Alec's front pockets right before a take. Believe me, Alec didn't think it was so damn funny.

The giant bear dies when he impales himself by falling on fire-hardened spears. In the next scene, the heroes appear, having skinned the bear and somehow managed to tan the hide and fashion it into bearskin coats with straight seams and lapels.

We left the Canadian Rockies with a deep friendship with "Tony" Hopkins. He served on the Vital Ground Foundation advisory board for years and narrated our first promotional video. Our dream that Bart's life in captivity had to matter for something more than movies was actually coming true. Vital Ground had an office and a two-person staff, and had helped tuck away a hundred thousand acres for wild creatures.

On our drive home, we stopped in the small town of Canmore at a gas station we had frequented when filming *Legends of the Fall*. Then we saw them: the old Stoney Elder and the girl. Her black braids were still shiny as a wet seal, but now her breast buds were tenderly swelling under her sweater. We were speechless, they had been waiting for us. The elder took her hand and came to the trailer door. She looked at Bart, then pressed a small, beaded leather bag into my hand. "I am well," was all she said. And then they left like grey smoke. I looked at the medicine bag; it had a bear paw against a ribbon sunrise that went from black to blue to purple to yellow. I keep the piece by my bed.

A Sunset and a Sunrise

We were a long way from "setback canyon" — now we were circling the mountaintop. Even before Bart's appearance at the Academy Awards, the phone would not stop ringing. We had calls from Discovery, National Geographic Television, Nova, CNN, NBC, and CBS. Bart was on a roll: *Inside Edition, Entertainment Tonight, The Today Show, 48 Hours, Jack Hanna's Into the Wild,* and *Lifestyles of the Rich and Famous*. (That last one cracked me up; it was filmed at our 1919 farmhouse with old pickup trucks in the background.) Articles on Bart appeared in magazines including *Backpacker, Outside, Architectural Digest, Life, National Geographic, Men's Health, Time*, and my personal favorite, *People*, where Bart was included among the 25 most beautiful people of the year. It was no surprise to us — he was our person, and he was beautiful.

That six-pound cub that I had whacked between the ears with a baby bottle now had to lower his bushel-basket head, just a bit, to rest his colossal chin on my chest as we rubbed noses. Bart and Doug

Bart the Bear giving me love c. 1998.

wrestled like Olympic champions (albeit of different weight classes). Yet he was forever gentle with me. And when I was away from set, he would follow Doug's instructions precisely, but a perceptible ease would descend on him like a warm honey when he saw me. He knew that mother grizzly protects her cubs.

In the summer of 1998, we were filming a silly Disney family comedy called *Meet the Deedles*. The film had a significant budget. The director, Steve Boyden, wanted to work with Bart and had created a cameo appearance for him as a circus bear. He had to wear a ridiculous array of hats, including a red-tasseled fez. No

Bart the Bear in *Meet the Deedles*. It was his last movie before being diagnosed with cancer.

problem; by now, Bart liked to wear hats. One scene called for Bart to stand upright and rock out with some teenagers at a party. For the first time in his 22 years, he had a bit of trouble standing to his full nine feet.

A few days later, during a morning romp and wrestle, Doug turned to me and said, "Bart has a lump on his wrist." Life as we knew it stopped. Our first call was to our local vet of many years. We knew his phone number by heart, as he did ours. Dr. Bruce

Williams arrived the next day with a field X-ray machine. Bruce gave Smitty the machine and instructed him how and when to fire it. Doug held the film plate behind Bart's leg while I gave him a can of iced tea to keep him in place. We went through several X-ray plates and lots of iced tea. Yes, there was a mass. It might be benign, but we needed a biopsy. We also needed a vet clinic with a huge, stainless-steel, hydraulic operating table, the kind used for 2,000-pound horses and prize bulls. We knew the place. It belonged to Dr. John Sieverts, a large animal vet who had tended to my horses for years and always stayed for a bit longer to look at our bears. We gathered a mighty team: three vets and two human physicians. One physician was a microvascular specialist, and the other was the best orthopedic surgeon in the state, Dr. Peter Stevens, who would remain in our lives and forever be known to us as "Saint Peter." The biopsy confirmed that the mass was a sarcoma, a monster with a logic of its own. At that time, there were three world-class animal cancer hospitals in the United States: one at Pennsylvania State University, another at the University of California, Davis, and a third at Colorado State University. We decided to take Bart to see the renowned Dr. Steven Withrow and his team of animal cancer specialists at the CSU Veterinary Teaching Hospital in Fort Collins. He did not seem to be in any pain, and the eight-hour drive from our valley to Colorado was lovely. We were so hopeful.

As usual, Smitty drove the truck and trailer while Doug and I followed behind in an SUV that could pull Bart's trailer if the truck ever broke down. "Saint Peter" met us there, taking time away from his busy practice while refusing to take a dime from us. The anesthesia, Carfentanil, was so powerful it was kept in a red box that required two different keys to open. One teaspoon in a cup of honey put Bart under. The anesthesiologist kept the reversal drug syringe in her hand. The team had never operated on a 1,500-pound Kodiak bear. It took the doctors several tries to find a vein for the IV. Veins lie deep below their skin — perhaps nature's way of protecting them from each other.

Our hope was for Dr. Withrow to excise the tumor — just

take the God damned thing out. Doug and I walked the halls outside the operating room. I remember the halls were painted a yellowish beige — I guess my mind had to go somewhere. During the procedure, a vet came out and asked us, "How would a three-legged bear make it?"

We collapsed. It was impossible to even consider such a thing. No. Never. To have him wake up without a front leg? Gnawing his stump? No. Never. "Sew him up," we said, "we'll take him home."

The doctors told us he had three months at most, as gently as they could. Smitty, Doug, and I held each other up as we sobbed.

Doug and I had followed that white 8' x 8' x 12' trailer for thousands of miles around the United States, Canada, and Western Europe for over 20 years. On the way home, we didn't say a word. We were each deep in our own quiet grief, our eyes fixed on the trailer, thinking about how our world was about to profoundly change. We stopped in Glenwood Springs, Colorado, to check on Bart. He seemed to have recovered from the anesthesia and looked hungry. Well, why not? We got him ten Big Macs, took out the pickles, and poured eight vanilla milkshakes into his water bucket — no reason to be concerned about a healthy weight now.

Then it occurred to me that for years I had "doctored" our family with holistic remedies, herbs, and essential oils. My kids were accustomed to mustard baths, raw garlic rubbed on the soles of their feet, and onion slices in their armpits. Osha root and olive leaf were standard issues in our home. Antibiotics were a desperate measure and rarely in the medicine chest.

"Three months," they had said, "there is nothing we can do." I might not help, but surely I would do no harm. I started researching, calling every naturopath and holistic doctor I could find. Our kitchen turned into Bart's healing center. We bought a commercial-grade juicer. Friends and family made daily runs to Whole Foods Market in Park City for all the bruised and blemished organic fruits and vegetables they would give us, and we juiced three times a day. Our kitchen counters were covered with amber bottles of tinctures and herbs, and beakers of soy protein isolate. We procured a mysterious

Bart the Bear's natural medicinal tinctures.

"black salve" from an old-time rancher in Idaho. Three months came, and three months went — he made it through the winter. The fur on his leg was growing back. The good vets at CSU said, "Whatever you're doing, just keep it up."

That spring, Doug and Bart did a public service spot for the Animal Cancer Center. (The blooper reel can be found on vitalground.org.) The video is funny and precious — Doug and Bart tumbling over each other as Doug tried to remember his lines — but also achingly sad, as it would be the last professional footage of them together.

A year had passed. The mass was back, a living monster the size of a football. Yet, there had been a medical advance — chemotherapy beads that could be inserted into the sarcoma. The second operation was more extensive, and the wound was larger. Once more, we followed the trailer west on Highway 40 toward home. It would be the last time. The chemo beads proved to be as useless as shotgun pellets on Godzilla. "It" was growing, and we could feel the new lumps on his neck ... children of the succubus.

Bart lay in the long grass by his pond. We gave him blueberries, ice cream, grilled cheese sandwiches, smoked salmon — anything that he wanted. One morning, he was sleeping on his belly when we took him his breakfast. He rolled onto his back and held his raw, bulging paw to our faces. We locked eyes. He moved it closer, almost touching us. He was telling us what we both already knew we must do for him.

It was hard to find my voice. "Dr. Bruce, it's Lynne calling. The time to help him leave is growing close. Bart told us so this morning. Yes, within the next couple of weeks. We will need to make arrangements with our Native Elders because there are songs and prayers for the passing of his spirit. We will arrange for the backhoe and have his grave ready ... I know, I know that you truly are, Bruce. Thank you." Doug and I were weeping, mostly inside, and the phone rang. I thought it was Dr. Bruce calling back.

"Hello," said a warm voice, "This is Kathy with the Alaskan Department of Fish and Game. We have two orphaned grizzly cubs in our office. Their mother was illegally shot last week. Our biologist, John Hechtel, thought you folks might be able to take them in. He said it would be a much better life for them by far than in any zoo. We can have a state trooper bring them down to you by Friday."

I was speechless. "Ah ... Eh, um ... Can we call you back, um, in a couple of hours? I mean this is a big decision."

"I totally understand," she said, "That would be great, thanks."

What had just happened? Doug and I looked at each other. We were in our early 50s. Jed and Sausha were away at college. Sure, we had Tank and the wolves and were not nearly ready to retire, but wild Alaskan brown bear cubs? The next 25 years of our lives would belong to them.

Well, of course we knew we would take them. Is that why we were given an extra year and three months with Bart? Why he had hung on so long? He waited until he knew there would be light in the abyss of our souls ... or at least we would be so busy that we would still see the horizon.

The Alaska state trooper, who looked like an Alaska state

trooper, arrived with an oversized dog crate. The orphans wore the white fur collars of baby bears. There was no doubt as to which one was the male; his head was already the size of a basketball. They had been with their mother for four months when she disappeared. Then, the human hand in the welding glove, the rope and net, the terrifying roar of the helicopter. Where was the silence that had surrounded them? Where was the soft, warm belly that had suckled them?

Would they ever be able to trust humans? We placed the cubs in a spacious enclosure with a kiddie pool, a tire swing, a huge doghouse with bedding hay, and a feed trough full of grapes and whipping cream. The date was April 15, and on May 1, Bart could not get up.

The cradle of earth we had dug to hold him was big enough for an SUV. We filled the bottom with white sage and aspen boughs

Bart the Bear's last days in his pond.

bursting their buds. Family and close friends gathered. Our Native Elders stood close with sweetgrass and ceremonial eagle wing fans. Dr. Bruce gave the syringe to Doug, who held Bart's massive head on his lap. The only thing Bart felt was Doug's arms around him. When the giant exhaled his last breath, Doug breathed it in ... deep, deep, deep down into his soul. There it remains. Doug gently closed Bart's still-shining amber eyes and covered them with his fleece jacket. He pulled off his medicine bag and wove it around the great, ivory claws. We all took turns with the shovels while the elders sang and prayed and saged us all with eagle wings.

Fly free, beloved.

We planted an apple tree on the mound of dirt and turned back to the waiting cubs.

Bart the Bear
1977-2000

Tiny five-pound cub asleep on our lap, soon only a small part of your massive head would fit there. Then for 23 years you took us on a grand adventure from the majestic peaks of the Austrian Alps and the Alaskan wilds, to the bejeweled backstage of the Academy Awards.

Just being, you were spectacular, with Doug you were magic. But your life in captivity had to matter for more than just movies, and your eyes ever spoke of the wild. So it would be we would work to save the wilderness you never knew.

Then there came others who understood the utter importance of this work and being able to stand in solitude, humbly before the great mystery of our first deity. The health of the unborn of all species is waiting.

As you died in our arms we were midwife to the rebirth of your great soul.

　　　　　　　　　　　　　　… run free Beloved Giant.

— Lynne Seus

Bart the Bear 2, Tank, and Honey-Bump

Wild Born

The mother grizzly sniffs the earth not far from her den. This should be the time for some tender greens. A shot from a high-powered rifle turns the snowbank crimson. The blast drives her cubs to the deepest recesses of the den. This is Alaska. The gutted bear is thrown into the back of a pickup truck. A state trooper spots the carcass in the truck bed outside a bar. The female's nipples are still swollen with milk. This is Alaska, with a stellar Fish and Game force. A dedicated biologist backtracks tire treads, footprints, and blood to the high and hidden den. The implausible destiny of these wild-born grizzlies will find them associating with some famous faces, and they will help save vanishing wild places.

Muskeg or Movie Sets

The Alaska Department of Fish and Game had named the little orphans Hoss and Honey. They were the size of English bulldogs but with better bone mass. There might be something cuter than a bear cub, but I can't remember what it is. We were busy with these wild ones from morning to night, but we were not too busy to grieve. Bart's big enclosure and den loomed, silent and empty, 15 feet from our back door. The grave mound of earth and rock was still damp and black with newness. The apple tree waved at us. But there was much to do. Bart, Zack, and Tank had been born in captivity. The new cubs had four months in the wild with their mother. The "mother substitute" of baby bottles is more easily accepted when the eyes of a cub are still sealed. These two new ones had their eyes wide open! They had known the "real deal." They had no use for that rubber thing on the end of a bottle — except it was fun to bite in half with their sharp, shiny, baby-grizzly teeth.

The most important element of bottle-feeding a wild animal is the cuddling and closeness, not the nutrition. These babies had no problem with nutrition — pans of cream, yogurt, grapes, peaches, and peanut butter and jelly sandwiches had them fat and sassy … mainly sassy. We needed the trust and bonding that bottle-feeding established. They were already five months old; we were behind in the "I am your friend" department.

We focused on establishing trust. One technique was to tie a rope between the legbones of a fat, yellow chicken and secure a tight knot for a firm handhold. Otherwise, there is no way to hang on to a slippery raw chicken if a bear cub is trying to pull it out of your hand. With the "rope trick," they must sit beside you and calmly gnaw the meat off the bone. Doug ended up with nine stitches in the ball joint of his right hand; I lucked out with only three on my arm. By June, they were learning to eat *out* of our hands without eating our hands.

We had never intended to call the male cub Bart, but the name kept slipping

Honey-Bump and Bart the Bear 2 bring joy and hope back to our family.

off our tongues as we played with him. We couldn't help it. His personality was identical, and he was a photocopy of Big Bart's baby pictures. He became known as Little Bart, that is, until he approached 1,000 pounds and simply became Bart (for movie credits, Bart the Bear 2). The female toddler soon renamed herself. She was a buzz bomb. She never walked anywhere; she ran, all the while bumping into everything — our Honey-Bump. Day by day, we gained their trust and affection.

I understood what a journey it had been for them. Three days had passed from the time their mother's body was confiscated until they were found. The Fish and Game biologist had searched long and hard for the remote den. The cubs were cold, hungry, and no doubt terrified when a human with welding-glove hands bound them with ropes and nets for the helicopter ride to Anchorage. The rescue saved their lives, but it took a while for them to be able to look calmly at a rope. The experience had surely bewildered them, but now they loved life with their play yard full of kiddie pools, sprinklers, and tire swings.

Early training with the cubs was brilliant. Young grizzlies are learning machines. With one of the longest childhoods in the animal kingdom, they spend two, sometimes three years with their mother learning what berries and roots to eat, what moths live under what rocks, which spot on what river belongs to whom, and what big male bears to stay away from. Standing upright for a cookie was pretty easy stuff. We started their socialization process. Rides to town always meant ice cream cones; trips to the mountains meant smashing watermelons and playing in creeks; construction sites meant picnics with tuna sandwiches and lemonade. Then, something wonderful happened that would be the best socialization and training we could ever have hoped for.

~~~~~~~~~~~~~~~~~~~~~~~~

Dr. Dolittle

There are only a few movies in which a bear is one of the star characters in almost every scene. *Dr. Dolittle 2*, starring Eddie Murphy, was one of those films. The prized role of Archie was given to our bear Tank.

Tank was born in captivity, but his lineage is that of the Lower 48 grizzly, the classic Yellowstone brown bear. There is something very special about Tank, beyond his handsome great and golden head. I think he is a Buddhist, and here is why. In our part of the Rockies, magpies, the black and white cousin of the crows of the Great Plains, are pesky and plentiful. They are clever birds, with one exception: when they sneak through an opening of a bear or wolf enclosure to steal a piece of chicken, they seem to have a hard time remembering where the door is. It doesn't take long for a lunch guest to become lunch. The outcome looks like the aftermath of a black-and-white pillow fight. That is, except for Tank. He receives his aerial visitors with gratitude as if to say, "Hello, my friend, how nice

Tank "discussing" a picture of a pretty female bear with Eddie Murphy in *Dr. Dolittle 2*.

of you to come and see me," as he sits calmly on his tractor-tire sofa and lets them feast on his leftover chicken.

With Tank the Bear under contract to 20th Century Fox, we set off for Los Angeles with the wild cubs in tow. The *Dr. Dolittle 2* storyline is really pretty cool. A rich and powerful logging company plans to clearcut a stand of old-growth forest, which is, of course, home to countless forest creatures. In the classic Dr. Dolittle tradition, the animals talk to the good doctor about their plight. The only hope for the salvation of the forest is to find an endangered species that lives there … and there is one, but just one, a lone female "Pacific western bear" named Ava. Hoping to form a breeding pair to save the forest, Dr. Dolittle locates the last surviving male of the species, a carnival bear named Archie. The fun begins as Archie goes from a bathtub in his dressing room to being reintroduced into the wild.

It is a gem of a family film, with enough one-line zingers to keep mom and dad laughing too. It was Tank's turn to shine — and shine he did. He sat in chairs and bathtubs and on a toilet. He rode on a motorcycle, danced a two-step sideways, did a running pratfall, ran a 100-yard dash with a fish in his mouth, and so much more, all while hitting every mark so the visual effects team could put Steve Zahn's voice in his mouth.

Little Bart and Honey-Bump were our constant companions during filming. What better place to train and socialize them than a movie set? The studio even wrote in a special scene for them. The wild ones had their first on-camera moment as Archie's and Ava's cubs disco dancing to the Bee Gee's "Stayin' Alive." No matter that in their playful curiosity they totally trashed all the Astroturf on the sound stage; they were superb.

Tank promoted the movie with an appearance on The Tonight Show, where he sat on the red guest sofa and leaned on Jay Leno's desk to "talk" with him. In all the publicity Tank did for the movie,

Little Bart and Honey-Bump's first big screen moment in *Dr. Dolittle 2*.

Doug as "Dan the Carnival Man" in *Dr. Dolittle 2*.

including spreads in *People Magazine* and *USA Today*, it never came out that deep down he was a Buddhist.

The year 2000 — the turning of a century. Computers were predicted to crash as their internal clocks reached the end of a millennium. Nothing much seemed to happen — but what a turning point it was for our family! We buried 24 years of our hearts and souls, and at the same time, we were blessed with Little Bart and Honey-Bump. And Tank became a star in his own right. We gave his earnings to The Vital Ground Foundation to save three estuaries in Alaska that were due to be turned into private salmon-fishing resorts and would be closed to local bears. The Sturgeon Lagoon in the Kodiak National Wildlife Refuge was preserved in Big Bart's name. The other two, on Yak Bay, were in honor of Tank and the nameless mother grizzly who had given birth to our wild ones.

~~~~~~~~~~~~~~~~~~~~~~~~~

Big Fish

If lucky stars are real, they were shining for us — our next film was *Big Fish*, directed by Tim Burton. Our family friend Arne Schmidt was the producer. This cinematic adventure did not include bears, but it gave our beautiful wolf pack a chance to shine. Beyond that, we were able to work together as a family. In addition to Doug, me, and Clint, Jed and Sausha were home from college and hired as film crew. Jed made his entrée into the camera department as a production assistant cleaning the camera truck and loading gear, while Sausha joined us as a wolf trainer. She had, after all, been raised by wolves. Her onscreen work for *Big Fish* would earn her membership in the Screen Actors Guild, and Jed continued on the path to becoming a successful Steadicam Operator for film and television.

We traveled to Alabama to film on an expensive circus set. The story was as bizarre as Tim Burton himself, and our part in the film remains one of the more peculiar of our careers. Danny DeVito's character, Amos Calloway, is a werewolf. He was played by our wolves in his animal form. One night, the werewolf attacks Edward Bloom, the main character played by Ewan McGregor, lunging for his neck. With the help of movie magic, Sausha doubled for Ewan in the fast-moving scene. Ewan then grabs a stick to defend himself, and suddenly the black werewolf wags his tail and wants to play fetch. Ewan gives the stick a mighty throw and the wolf happily retrieves it, bouncing over two cars, which in reality were green boxes in front of a green screen. At dawn, Amos Calloway turns back into a human. In the last shot of the scene, Danny was butt-naked, scratching his ear with his foot — pure Tim Burton.

Tim Burton wanted the werewolf to all be black. At that time, we had only one black color phase wolf in our pack, Shadow. However, the wolf work was demanding so we brought along three grey wolves: Legend, Koda, and Yukon. The first order of business on shoot days was to fill a sprayer with temporary hair color and cover their light fur. The product was made for human hair and was easily

Sausha filming on a green screen with our wolf Shadow for *Big Fish*.

washed out. The wolves seemed to find it cool and refreshing.

The set was so expansive that the cast and crew were given four wheelers to get around. The only four-wheeler that had no speed governor, but was super-charged, belonged to Burton. He always wore round blue glasses and a long cape that would fly behind him as he raced through set. He would screech to a halt at our wolf camp and say, "They give me the shivers," then jet away.

It was truly wonderful to be working with our family, and what memories we share from our time together on *Big Fish*.

Grizzlies Growing Up

Dan Arden was one of the most genuine people we had ever met. He had the gentleness of Tank. Slight of build, with prematurely snow-white hair, a boyish face with pink cheeks under soft blue eyes. He came to us with a project he had created for Animal Planet called *Growing Up Grizzly*. The budget was minuscule, but we were intrigued by the possibility that the concept would help raise awareness of America's dwindling and isolated populations of grizzly bears. The script would follow Little Bart and Honey-Bump's unlikely journey, from their rescue in Alaska to their first birthday and into early training. We were determined to include the conservation work of the Vital Ground Foundation. Then the word came down from the Discovery headquarters in New York: There was to be absolutely no mention of or promotion of Vital Ground. It might piss off the logging, mining, and oil companies. ... We remembered a certain superstar from

Tank with Doug and Brad Pitt filming the first *Growing Up Grizzly*.

Legends of the Fall who had said, "Let me know if I can ever help with your work for wild bears." Doug made a call. The next day, we got back to Discovery. "What if we could bring you Brad Pitt as a narrator ... at no charge?" Their reply was, "Well then, you can mention anything you want to."

True to his word, the megastar took time off right in the middle of filming *Ocean's Eleven*. His private plane flew into the Provo Airport, where Doug met him in our old pickup. I suppose the movie's producers were none too happy that their billion-dollar face was taking leave to spend time with grizzly bears.

I had made chicken and fairy-ring mushroom soup, and we planned the shoot over dinner. The next thing I knew, Brad Pitt was in the kitchen doing dishes (someone had raised him well). The following day, he hung out with Tank, nose-to-nose, and played with the cubs. That evening, seated in front of our fireplace in a gray V-neck sweater, Brad did a public service spot for The Vital Ground Foundation, which can still be seen online. Vital Ground's membership went through the roof.

For some people, their word is their honor. Brad's honor was a priceless gift to the conservation of wild things and their wild places.

~~~~~~~~~~~~~~~~~~~~~~~

An Unfinished Life

We were leaning on a fence rail with Robert Redford, who we knew as Bob by that time. The conversation was about a grizzly bear long gone but not forgotten by any of us. "Willie the Wonder Bear" had chased Bob up a tree and shredded his pant leg (unscripted) while filming *Jeremiah Johnson*. The same bear Doug had wrestled for the cover photo of our first brochure in 1977. It was a soft summer day in 2003 on the set of *An Unfinished Life*. Doug had shaved his beard, and the makeup department had dyed his hair and eyebrows a sandy red so he could double the famous actor for the stunts in the film. The two men looked remarkably alike as

Doug doubles as Robert Redford taking a hit from Bart the Bear 2 in *An Unfinished Life*.

they reminisced. The set was in Kamloops, B.C., Canada. The landscape, which Canadians call their "desert," looked more like Wyoming than Wyoming itself. The grey-green foothills were covered with aspen, spruce, and Douglas fir. Bart was cast to play the bear in the screenplay of Mark Spragg's compelling novel, *An Unfinished Life*.

Redford's character, Einar Gilkyson, has never recovered from the death of his son, who was killed in an auto accident. His daughter-in-law Jean, played by Jennifer Lopez, had been driving. For twelve years, Einar has hated her deeply. The only stable element in Einar's life is his longtime ranch hand, Mitch, played by Morgan Freeman, who had been mauled badly by a bear a year earlier trying to save a calf. Jean and her eleven-year-old daughter Griff, played by Becca Gardner, are trying to escape an abusive boyfriend. The only place they have to run to is Einar's ranch. His first words to Jean are, "I don't want you here," but upon seeing his granddaughter for the first time, he tells Jean she can stay until she finds someplace else to hide.

Mitch is maimed, disabled, covered with scars, and in constant pain from the bear attack. The bear had been captured and is now in a shabby roadside zoo, where he is gawked at by the locals.

When Mitch is finally able to walk, he visits the bear in his cramped steel and concrete cage. Mitch later begs Einar to "let the bear go." In the dead of night, the old man and his granddaughter crank open the bear's cage. Then the truck slips out of gear, and Bart has his first major motion picture moment. It was a tough one. He had to do a running, rib-breaking scene with Doug as Einar, then immediately stop and stand, poised to kill. Back in the truck, the young girl leans on the horn at that precise moment. Bart does a running exit over the hills.

With the release of the bear, Einar releases his bitter hatred as he lies in the hospital, healing his ribs and his heart with Jean and Griff by his side.

The medicine bear has one more stop to make. One night when Mitch is outside the ranch house, he meets the bear face to face again. It is a powerful scene as Mitch faces his fear and forgives the bear.

Morgan Freeman did his own scene. When Bart strikes the ground

Robert Redford and Becca Gardener with Bart the Bear 2 on the set of *An Unfinished Life*.

at his feet the flying gravel hits Morgan in the chest. Doug is kneeling just out of frame behind a shed. Morgan said to him as Bart approached him, "You got me covered, don't you, man?" Morgan Freeman is an amazing actor and a wonderful human being.

Bart was only three years old then, and rather like a twelve-year-old boy. He still had the panda-rings of cubhood around his eyes and had reached only 1,000 of the 1,500 pounds he would expand to. If his destiny had been to grow up in Alaska, he most likely would have been spending his first summer on his own, maybe still hanging out with his sibling, as bears often do. Instead, his mother's senseless death had landed him on a movie set with some of Hollywood's finest. The young grizzly had nailed it. He could not have been better. We were so proud and grateful for him.

Let me share something special that happened at the end. We were wrapped and in the process of packing the gear away just so, for the customs inspection that would take place at the border crossing on the way home. A call came over the walkie talkie. "Could the Seuses return to set to discuss a pick-up shot?" What? Ah, geez … Oh well, we wanted everything to be perfect for Bart's first big feature. We trekked back to set, where the entire cast and crew stood outside the ranch house. Whooping shouts, cheers, and a standing ovation led by Bob Redford and Morgan Freeman. It was all for Doug, who had to shake his head and pinch his eyebrows to stop the tears before he could manage to say thank you.

A parcel of land in Montana conserved by The Vital Ground Foundation in 2021. Where the grizzly can walk, the Earth is healthy and whole.

Bart was just as good as Tank about handing over his paycheck to Vital Ground. His first purchase was an 80-acre parcel in Montana called Coyote Forest that would remain forever wild.

Our next adventure would carry us as far away from home as possible on planet Earth.

A Grizzly in Middle Earth

Paramount Pictures hired us for an outrageous comedy about three 20-something men who reconnect after the death of a boyhood friend and are determined to fulfill their teenage dream of a shared wilderness adventure. None of them had any experience in the outdoors. They are up the proverbial creek *Without a Paddle* when their canoe takes a dive over a waterfall. Lucky for us, a big bear lives on the same creek.

The wacky wilderness comedy starring Seth Green, Matthew Lillard, and Dax Shepard takes place in the deep *"Deliverance"* woods of the South but would be shot in New Zealand. Bart the Bear had flown across the Atlantic; now, his namesake would take the longest flight ever taken by a grizzly bear. Bart remains the only grizzly bear ever to have left a track in the land of the Kiwis.

I looked at the old, sage-green library globe in our front room. I always found it fascinating because it was made in the 1920s when the borders of many countries had been freshly carved by the blood, bombs, and barbed wire of World War I, but not yet rearranged by World War II. That day, I had to tip my head down to look for New Zealand. If I skewered the globe, stabbing the ball like a marshmallow through Utah, the tip of the skewer would come out through New Zealand. It was on the other side of the world, as far away as we could go without starting to circle back home.

New Zealand is environmentally pristine. For that, "Good on ya, mates." There are no snakes or even poisonous spiders, and they wish to keep it that way. A visitor's luggage is thoroughly inspected for so much as an apple seed. The crevices of sneakers are checked for mud that might contain invasive weed seeds. The economic benefit of a big Hollywood production notwithstanding, I can imagine the Minister for the Environment saying to Paramount, "You want to bring in a what?!"

We traveled by truck to Los Angeles International Airport, where the trailer and tires were power washed, and Bart was bedded in certified-sanitized wood chips. The carrier was a Singapore Jumbo Cargo Jet. An enormous scissor lift gently settled the trailer into the cargo hold. Inside the pressurized, air-conditioned hold, the dimly lit atmosphere hummed with white noise. Actually, the sound was peacefully relaxing compared to the Los Angeles freeways we had been traveling. The huge jet had only five seats and bunks behind the pilot and co-pilot — just enough for us and a French gentleman who was accompanying a precious piece of art sealed in foam and double-crated in the cargo hold with Bart. I fantasized about what was inside that crate. A da Vinci? A Titian? A Van Gogh?

The route to New Zealand made an arc around the planet — flying over Los Angeles, Anchorage, Seoul, Singapore, and Sidney along the way. The flight took 36 hours. There was a small door at the back of the flight deck where a winding steel staircase led down to the cargo hold. We had brought along a case of Gatorade, dried apricots, and granola bars, but when we offered Bart snacks, he would crack open one eye, roll over, and go back to sleep like ... a bear.

We landed in Auckland and went through customs. We knew we could have absolutely no agricultural material of any kind in our luggage. We took off our jackets and shoes for inspection. Then, a loud *beep beep beep* — Doug's hiking boots had bits of mud deep in the crevices of the rubber soles. The boots were whisked away for sanitation. Doug stood barefoot as he was handed his $250 "dirtball fine."

We scurried back to the jumbo jet. A forklift that could easily have handled a Sherman tank was waiting to unload Bart, who had thoroughly enjoyed his long nap in the soft, sanitized wood chips. We had to wait our turn at the decontamination station, a large, dish-shaped concrete pad with a drain hole in the center. It was like a giant garbage disposal. Ahead of us, a FedEx crate containing four prize Hanoverian show horses was being power-washed. Bart's trailer was next. After shoveling out the wood chips, we washed Bart and the trailer. He loved it. It was December, summer in New Zealand.

The Ministry for the Environment had slapped strict rules on us. Bart was to be kept in his trailer until we reached the movie location, which was a lovely, privately owned farm in Wairarapa on the North Island. The ministry had seen to it that the four-strand electric fence (common on sheep ranches all over New Zealand) was extended around the farm's perimeter and in perfect working order. They had also insisted that a veterinarian armed with a high-powered tranquilizer gun stand by whenever Bart was outside his trailer. That lasted for about a day. When the armed security vet saw Bart tumbling around with Doug in the hay fields with spikes of purple foxgloves that grow all over New Zealand, he returned to his car, where he slept through his guard duty that day, which he continued to do for the rest of the shoot.

Our first shot was at night. Like his namesake, Bart 2 always loved working and being the center of attention. He eagerly hopped out of his trailer and then stopped abruptly at his first view of the sparkling night sky. He craned to look up where the North Star should have been, looked over his shoulder at us, and turned again to ponder the unfamiliar constellations of the Southern Hemisphere. I don't know if a biologist has ever studied whether bears use the night sky to guide their treks, but I watched Bart consider deeply the stars before him. Was he searching for his star map to navigate home in case he had to walk there?

Bart's big scene takes place on the friends' first night in the wilderness. After a few beers, Dax Shepard's character decides to night fish with a flashlight and his hand. As he passes a second fish to his buddies, he notices a look of horror on their faces and turns to find himself face-to-face with a towering Bart. All turn and run. The phobia-ridden, hypochondriac physician Dan, played by Seth Green, lags behind his two companions and stumbles. His buddies yell at him to assume the fetal position! He does so as he sobs, but then Bart sniffs and licks him from head to toe, picks him up by the belt, and carries him off to "her" den. The bear thinks the tiny man is her cub! After being plopped into the den, Seth remains frozen with fear in the fetal position. The bear leaves briefly and returns with a rabbit, guts exposed (a prop, of course), to nourish her still sobbing cub. The buddies, peeking over a rock into the den, whisper loudly that he must eat it, which he does (and pukes). When the mother bear goes to find him another rabbit, the two pals then help the "cub" out of the bear den and into a tree that towers above their campsite. The mother bear is not happy about losing her cub and trashes the campsite as the guys spend the night in the tree.

Doug and Bart the Bear 2 prepping at home with Seth Green's dummy for *Without a Paddle*.

Bart was like a kid at Christmas ripping apart the campsite. When he poked his head into a blue cooler, it got stuck, really stuck. He wandered about blind-man's-bluff style until he finally sat down and popped the damned thing off with his claws. The crew split their sides with laughter. It could have never been scripted, but it was all caught on film and made it into the movie — a gift to the director, Steve Brill.

After being there for a month, I had no doubt why the director of *The Lord of the Rings* demanded the landscape of New Zealand, which is otherworldly in its mystery. Hobbits could live nowhere else. (I know I saw one, but I was afraid to say anything). Beyond the incredible landscape were the Maori people. Our driver was an Indigenous fellow named Ardy. We learned that in the Maori culture, one does not drive without singing, and when it is your turn to "give a song," it would be rude not to pipe up.

The Maori farm where we were quarantined became our home; their family became our family, and their kitchen table was our table. When it was time to leave New Zealand, the matriarch gathered us in a circle. "Take off your shoes and stand on the earth," she said. We held hands, and she prayed in her mother tongue for our safety on the long journey home.

Smoothly, we arced over the planet back to the Rocky Mountains, but it took a while for us to come down from the magic and beauty of New Zealand, and the people who had entered our spirits like a barbed arrow that could not be removed.

In His Own Footprints

The summer the wild-born bear guy turned five, he was over 1,000 pounds and well on his way to his adult weight of 1,300. Standing upright, he was every bit as tall as his namesake at 9 feet and 3 inches, but he was finer-boned. His limbs were aspens; Big Bart's had been ponderosa pines. The orphaned cubs had been born 150 miles from the coast. Biologists consider them interior brown bears, *Ursus arctos horribilis*. (I always wondered who came up with the name horribilis) Big Bart was *Ursus arctos middendorffi*, a Kodiak whose DNA was from the island of that name in the Aleutian Archipelago. His top weight was 1,580 pounds. However, 200 pounds less bear mass did not limit the younger bear's budding career.

During a lifetime with bears, you come to realize that their faces are distinct and as easily recognizable as human faces. Big Bart was dubbed by many directors the "John Wayne of Bears." His handsome namesake could be called the "George Clooney of Bears." Young Bart's coat is a shining, rim-fire of golden brown. He always seems to be backlit, no matter what the camera angle. For all his gold, his sister Honey-Bump is pure silver. Her undercoat is dark sable, highlighted by long guard hairs tipped in Tiffany platinum — a classic silvertip. I wondered about the mother of these bears, selectively bred by nature's finest and fittest; was she gold or silver? My guess is she was a silvertip who wandered west one spring and met a big, brawny, golden male. I had done the same.

That summer, we were blessed with the exquisite presence of Jennifer Aniston, who had volunteered to host *Growing Up Grizzly 2*. She opened the show by referring to her then-husband, Brad Pitt, who had hosted *Growing Up Grizzly*, saying, "Why should he have all the fun?" Both Doug and Bart fell madly in love with her. Who can blame them? So did I. What was there not to love? Holding Bart's pillow-size paw between her slender hands, she gave voice to Vital Ground when she said, "This species has a right to exist." With her support, Vital Ground's membership and mission of protecting and connecting wildlife corridors deepened and widened.

Bart the Bear 2 admires Jennifer Aniston as she films *Growing Up Grizzly 2*.

~~~~~~~~~~~~~~~~~~~~~~

Did You Hear About the Morgans?

Bart continued appearing in commercials, documentaries, television shows, and movies. One of his roles was in *Did You Hear About the Morgans?*, a fluff of a comedy starring Hugh Grant, Sara Jessica Parker, Sam Elliot, and Mary Steenburgen. The location was Val Kilmer's ranch on the banks of the Pecos River in New Mexico. We stayed in an adobe guesthouse a short walk from the main set, which was Kilmer's big-timbered ranch house. Bart's trailer was parked in the shade of a cedar tree a few feet from our bedroom window. It was a dream location. The soft, red earth glittered with chipped flakes of agate, flint, and chalcedony. Native potsherds were scattered about like puzzle pieces — the ancient presence on the land beside the river was palpable.

Hugh and Sara Jessica portray a wealthy New York socialite couple. Leaving a restaurant after celebrating the three-month anniversary of their separation, they witness a gruesome murder and lock eyes with the professional killer. The assassin learns who they are and where they live. The FBI places the couple in a witness protection program in a speck of a town in Wyoming under the protection of the local lawman, who is played by Sam Elliott, and his wife and pistol-packin' deputy, played by Mary Steenburgen.

The estranged couple are out for a morning run when they are surprised by a bear. Screaming in terror, they run for their lives. Sara Jessica makes it back to the ranch house first, where she frantically searches for the "Bear Away" pepper spray. Hugh is paralyzed by indecision between the door of the ranch house and the big bear. The Englishman, in his fumbling, bumbling way has a face-to-face talk with the bear, saying things like, "Oh, hello there, how are you? May I say that I am not a hunter, uhhh, I don't even own a gun… I want you to know I am a wilderness advocate, uhhh, actually, I live in New York City."

Bart played his part well, cocking his head at the man as if he were completely crazy. Hugh makes a run for the door, and Sara Jessica manages to spray "Bear Away" directly in Hugh's eyes as he lunges into the house. The bear shakes his head in amusement and ambles off.

Hugh Grant was terrific to work with. In a behind-the-scenes trailer at the end of the film, he is interviewed about his scene with Bart and says that the bear is really a bit "Queenie" because the big beast had to be bathed, brushed, and given a saucepan of whipped cream before each of his scenes like royalty. "He was treated much better than most of the crew." Of course he was.

Doug and Sam Elliott hit it off like two old fishing buddies swapping stories and dipping Copenhagen on the tailgate of a pickup. I was dumbfounded around that man and could not think of one intelligible thing to say, so I just looked at my feet … the only time I have ever been starstruck. Despite my sophomoric stupor, the friendship between Sam and Doug was instant and natural. Sam agreed to do a public service announcement for Vital Ground. The deep, chocolaty voice of the classic cowboy speaking up for bears and wildlife still plays on NPR and can be found on Vital Ground's website.

~~~~~~~~~~~~~~~~~~~~~~

Evan Almighty

We were again at Universal Studios, this time for a big-budget Noah's Ark movie with a huge cast, *Evan Almighty*, starring Steve Carell and our friend Morgan Freeman, who, of course, plays God. Carell's character, Evan Baxter, is a pretentious, newly elected Republican Congressman. God suddenly appears, in a white T-shirt, in the back seat of Baxter's car and commands him to build an ark.

For the first part of the film, we crossed the country with our wolves to Charlottesville, Virginia. Clint, Smitty, and Sausha handled the wolves for that part of the shoot where the cast of animals was loaded, two at a time, into the ark. Bart's scene was on the Universal lot in Los Angeles, where we joined forces with what seemed like almost every other animal trainer on the planet. The scenes with the ark animals were all on blue screen, split screen, motion control, or some other computer-generated imagery. How else could there be lions, giraffes, hyenas, bears, elephants, sheep, snakes, and water buffalo in the same scene? The ark was built inside a stadium-sized soundstage. Bart was terrified by the huge dangling air conditioning tubes that rippled like blue cobras. The entire soundstage was scented with pee from every exotic animal species in the film. It was one damn scary place!

Bart played both bear roles for "two by two they came." Bravely, he made his way up the ramp into the ark and turned right into his (their) chamber. Bart soldiered through for us, even though his highly evolved, Northern Hemisphere brain was not wired for elephants, water buffalo, hyenas, and the like. He was as happy as we were to move on to our next job.

Back Into the Wild

The movie bear world is small. We became aware of a bear scene in the film version of *Into the Wild*, John Krakauer's best-selling account of the adventures of wayfaring Christopher McCandless. That time, we did the calling. The film's director was cinematic genius Sean Penn. The iconic cast featured Emile Hirsch, Catherine Keener, and Hal Holbrook. The bear scene was short but powerful. The story, the actors, the location, and the director had the makings of a classic. We called the production manager and basically begged to be part of the film. We would work for minimum wage on a Screen Actors Guild stunt coordinator's contract for Doug. Bart would come along for the ride — and what a ride it was. It would be our longest overland journey — a 6,000-mile round trip from Utah to the Canadian town of Cantwell, at the terminus of the Denali Highway on the banks of the Susitna River.

Bart always liked to go places. The only thing is, he liked to look out the window the whole time. Our family cannot be without dogs, and we always have two or sometimes three at a time (I cannot imagine sleeping well without a dog at my feet). Some of our dogs curl up and snooze away car rides; others have to look out the window to make sure they don't miss anything. That is how Bart traveled, looking out the back and side trailer windows. Our eight-foot-tall bear trailer is as generic as we could make it. Passengers in cars could not see the huge teddy bear ears and eyes peeking out. But when passing truckers glanced over, their brake lights flashed as they slowed down to be sure of what they saw. Occasionally, a long hauler would follow us to a gas stop. The usual questions were, "Where the hell did you catch him?" or "Is that Bart the Bear?" It put light and laughter into road trips.

After Edmonton began the unbelievable Alcan Highway; signs there warned, "Next gas station 250 miles." For hours upon hours, we would not see another car. As much as he loved traveling, we could not ask Bart to stay in his trailer for six long days (one way), and we never traveled more than six to eight hours a day. We had charted motels and gas stations along the desolate route. A crowd of onlookers would always gather at our gas stops, and we would explain that the huge grizzly in the trailer was headed to a movie set, and then we would ask, "Say, does anyone happen to have a backyard (on the Alcan, folks have football field-sized backyards) where we can set up our little wire fence and let our bear stretch his legs for a bit?" Every hand would shoot into the air. "Mine!" "Mine's bigger!" "I'll make coffee!" Wherever we landed, all the neighbors in their rubber knee-high boots and Helly Hansen jackets gathered to watch. There was always coffee and, most of the time, cookies for both us and Bart.

At one stop, by Whitehorse, in Yukon Territory, the locals welcomed Bart in a lovely yard under pine trees. He was alternating rolling on his back and chomping grass when a Boreal toad the size of a thumbnail jumped on him. Imagine a tarantula jumping on a four-year-old boy. He let out a woof and jumped up and back three feet in the air. He looked around him again, and they were all over the place — hundreds hopping and jumping. I can't think what would have happened if one had landed on his nose. His bear lips were pursed in an "O" as he ran to Doug for protection. The onlookers were hanging onto each other laughing as Doug caught one of the tiny amphibians in his palm to show Bart that it was "nice." Never mind! He didn't believe Doug and headed for the apples and hay in his trailer.

The coolest thing about the spacious motel grounds along the Alcan was that we could back the trailer right up to our motel door.

Bart would peek right into our room and watch TV with us. At one motel in Fort St. John, there was a grassy strip perfect for stretching and grazing (we checked for toads first). We asked the motel owner, who said, "Of course." As the townspeople and local newspaper started to gather with excitement, the rotund motel owner took charge, even of the four "Dudley-Do-Right" Mounties who had joined the crowd. He raised his authoritarian voice and said, "This is one of God's greatest creatures. Act like you're in church." They did. The next day, in the Fort St. John news, there was a picture of Bart and a headline that read, "Famous Movie Star Visits Fort St. John." We still have the newspaper pressed in an archival folder, and the memory is pressed in my heart.

The shoot location was on the wilderness side of the Susitna River. Production had built a small, two-board track bridge over the river. Okay for small 4x4s to cross, but we had to ford the river. We

Bart the Bear 2, on the set of *Into the Wild*, only 55 miles from his birth den in the wilds of Alaska.

nested Bart and his trailer in a stand of bottlebrush spruce trees a half-mile across the tundra. When he put his foot on the deep sponge floor of the muskeg, he was only 55 miles from the den where he had been born. I truly believe he sensed it; surely the smell was familiar. It was August, and the undulating ground was covered with knee-high blueberry bushes. He rolled over and over, nibbling as he went until he came to a spruce tree. Delighted, he gave it a hug. I imagined him saying, "Well, hey, these things just pop right out." Bottlebrush spruce have roots like a hair net that clings to the tender, seafoam soil just above the permafrost.

Bart was six years old. What if his mother had not been shot? Would he perhaps have been in the same spot, feeding on blueberries and seeking a mate? Or would he have become a trophy hanging on the wall of someone's man cave?

Setting up our perimeter fence, I realized as I stepped up and over the sofa-pillow heaves of the muskeg why winter is the only time to travel by land there. The brambles and scrambles can't grab and tear your legs in winter because one travels on open roads in sleds pulled by winged huskies.

Bruce, the production assistant assigned to us, was a tall, big-boned, rugged, Athabaskan Native. He invited us to his nearby home for coffee. Inside the sturdy wooden house, the walls, floors, and furniture were draped with golden grizzly bear hides, half of them from cubs. "I have killed over 40 of them," he said matter-of-factly. In certain areas of Alaska, it is open season on bears 365 days a year. I dug my nails deep into my palms to keep my mouth shut. We were in his house, and it was his culture.

On set the next day, Doug asked Bruce to stand very close, eye-to-eye, to Bart in his trailer. A huge tongue slipped between the bars and licked the man's face from chin to forehead. Stunned silence. Then Bruce said softly to Bart, "I will never kill you again."

The story of Christopher McCandless, who called himself Alexander Supertramp, was digested, dissected, and masterfully reassembled by Sean Penn. Most of the crew, including us, had worked for Sean before, and once you work for the man, you are forever devoted to him.

Emile Hirsch became McCandless. Not having an extra ounce of fat on his body to begin with, he lost 40 pounds to reenact the death by starvation of McCandless. Hirsch was kept in a separate tent between scenes under a doctor's care. In the encounter with the grizzly, McCandless is dying and delusional. The human and the bear were inches apart. There was no split screen, no computer graphics; it was a real encounter directed by Sean Penn, who would have it no other way. Hirsch felt Bart's breath on his chest as they questioned each other's existence. It was one of the most powerful moments we have ever put on film.

As we filmed, the skies deepened and darkened into leaden layers. Once it started to rain, it did not stop. Then, our own adventure drama began. Sean and his team listened to the locals who listened to the river, and decided to prioritize Bart's scenes. The autumnal rains had turned the Susitna into the same roaring river that had trapped and dissolved Alexander Supertramp. By late August, it was clear we could not wait out the rains. If we didn't cross

Monster trucks ferrying the bear trailer across the swollen Susitna River after filming *Into the Wild*.

soon, we would be on the wilderness side until summer or until the Army Corps of Engineers could build a big bridge across the mighty river, which would keep raging higher and higher through spring. The production assistants were local Alaskans who all drove "monster trucks" with wheels taller than my head. Knowing the water would engulf our truck's engine, we pulled out the battery and cabled our truck and Bart's trailer, front and back, to the massive trucks. Even so, the trailer fish-tailed, and the Susitna kissed Bart's belly. It could have gone horribly wrong.

    The 3,000-mile trip back home was lovely as we passed through the endless wildness of the Yukon, stopping along the way at the backyards of our new "old friends."

The Old Man and The Bear

February 20, 2012, seven months and 18 days until his 70th birthday. He is feverishly, intensely focused. His hearing is under the earmuffs of age. He limps a little on his right ankle that was broken in a high school football game. He has sprained it so many times since, that it looks like he is smuggling a softball inside his ankle. His head juts forward a bit now. But at the call, "Camera is ready," 30 years are whisked away by the magician's trick of pride. Doug squares his still burly shoulders and stands tall, as if trying to reach the six feet one-half inch he always said he was. As Bart comes out of his trailer, the massive bear senses that this is not the usual "stand up and open your mouth" stuff. His old friend is wearing a sheriff's jacket. His graying hair is sprayed totally white to match the actor's.

Doug starts the stunt by standing, slapping on his chest, and telling Bart to "wrestle." Bart's eyes light up. Wham! He charges Doug and sends him sailing five feet through the air, then body slams on top of him. Doug disappears under a mass of brown-gold fur, flat on the ground. The camera sees a flailing arm, a kicking leg, and then a face that screams, "Wrestle, wrestle!"

Bart pins him with one huge paw and shreds the sheriff's jacket. Doug commands "Easy," and the giant lets up and returns to take the smiling, wrinkled face gently in his mouth. The director is ecstatic. I watch, not really breathing, as I have watched so many times before. One misplaced six-inch fang, one misplaced claw in an eye, one crush on a spleen ... I know these things.

But I trust in this relationship between a bear-hearted human and a human-hearted bear.

Doug goes to the edge of the cliff and, once again ... he flies.

Doug and Bart the Bear 2 show the trust possible between a man and bear (2015).

Lions and Tigers and Bears in Downtown Boston and Elsewhere

Bart's career continued to flourish. His television credit list was growing as large as his namesake's, including episodes of *The Amazing Race, CSI, Good Morning America, Sixty Minutes Australia*, and so many more. There were also dozens of movies, from small-budget independents to big-budget studio blockbusters. Some were mindless and silly, some were award-winning masterpieces, and some were too horrible to mention (even the one with an A-list star and astonishing bear work). Three films stand out above the rest.

Big Bart was never called upon to work with lions, so I don't know what his reaction would have been to the reverberating, soul-shaking roar of the "king of beasts." The Romans pitted lions against the brown bears of Europe in the Colosseum. Pliny, writing in the 2nd century A.D., reveals that only one animal could best a bear, and it was not a lion. But our *Ursus arctos* did not like them one damned bit, and he had to share three major motion pictures with them. We had made it through *Evan Almighty* with its big cats, and now on our plate was a thick script from MGM Studios that called for lions and tigers and bears: *Zookeeper*, starring Kevin James. Filming was to take place in Boston.

Knowing how Bart felt about the sound, sight, and smell of big cats, we might have passed but for one thing: the script called for two bears. It would be Honey-Bump's chance to shine her silver. She would share a single-card, front-end credit with her brother. Because the project required both bears and nearly twice the work, Jed joined us in Boston to help.

Zookeeper, like *Dr. Dolittle 2*, was a Looney Tunes-style talking animal script with the voices of Nick Nolte, Sylvester Stallone, Adam Sandler, and Cher. Bart and Honey-Bump played two teenage brothers, Jerome and Bruce, who were constantly giving each other crap and wrestling like Japanese Sumos. One of Jerome's lines was, "I just peed in your water bucket." Bruce replies, "What the hell? You told me they were vitamins," and the wrestling match is on.

No matter how worried Bart was about the lions next door, Bump could not have cared less about the big cats (probably because she knew she could take them out). She would whack Bart upside his head as if to say, "Get over it," and if he didn't, she would whack him again and again until all he could do was wrestle her back.

MGM had created its own zoo adjacent to the Franklin Park Zoo in an old, Victorian section of Boston that had since become the inner city. The movie set was separated from the real zoo by a chain-link-and-canvas fence. The holding area for the movie animals was in what remained of an old-growth forest of giant sycamore trees, with ground covered in lush green plants, mainly poison ivy. Doug was the only one who succumbed to the three-leafed scourge.

During our second night shooting, I asked a security guard, "How is it that there are so many tire blowouts in this area?" He tilted his head and looked at me as if I were a child. "Miss Lynne, those are gunshots." Well now, I had been to The United Kingdom, all over Europe, Africa, Mexico, Canada, Samoa, the Caribbean, Central America, and New Zealand, but suddenly I felt like I had never been outside of Table Rock, Nebraska. Now I understood the note on the call sheet that said to travel with a full tank of gas, and if we experienced car trouble, to stay in our car and call production immediately. Indeed, it was a world apart for our wild-born Alaska grizzlies.

We usually filmed at night because, according to the story, midnight was when the zoo animals could begin talking to each

Bart the Bear 2 on the set of *Zookeeper*.

other. The climactic animal scene in the film takes place one night in the center of the zoo. Crystal, the world-famous Capuchin monkey, steals the zookeeper's keys and unlocks all the exhibits. The zoo creatures have a meeting about helping the zookeeper, Kevin James, win the love of his life.

The scene was a technical accomplishment rendered by master visual effects artists in a control booth — it was extremely difficult to execute. The animals had to be precisely on their marks. A voice would come over the walkie-talkie from one of the techs in the video control room trying to fit all the giraffes, elephants, lions, wolves, and bears in the same scene. "Please move Bart over six inches to his right." Six inches? Holy crap, if he breathes, he moves six inches! It was exacting and demanding work.

One would have thought that after 30 years of training bears, we would never find ourselves trying to catch a loose grizzly. That would all change in Boston. We usually rehearsed in the late afternoon when the animals could see their surroundings in natural light. One afternoon, "Tank the Gentle" was spending time on set. The movie zoo's bear exhibit featured a moat dressed with a bit of a pier, an old rowboat, and fishing nets. Smitty had the bright idea to prepare Tank for surprises, which always seemed to happen on set. He snuck under one of the fishing nets in the moat and rose up from the water like a swamp monster. Tank saw the "creature from the black lagoon," and with a look of pure terror, jumped across the moat and over the movie set perimeter's chain-link fence — he was getting the hell out of there, even if he didn't know where he was going. Actually, he was running free in the very public Franklin Park Zoo. Lucky for us, there were lots of trees to obscure our loose grizzly bear and the three frenzied trainers chasing behind him. He stopped short when he saw the African wild dog exhibit and was glad to see us (sans swamp monster). Doug and Smitty led him back through the woods. As I walked behind them with an oak branch covering up the tracks, I said to myself "this never happened, this never happened, this never happened." We didn't tell a soul.

    We were housed at the Liberty Hotel, set between the Charles River and the Boston Commons in the center of downtown Boston. It was only a short stroll from Beacon Hill and Paul Revere's house, which I relished. The luxurious hotel was originally the Charles Street Jail, designed by the famed architect Gridley Bryant and built in 1851. It had held some of Boston's most notorious criminals but was closed in 1973 because the deplorable living conditions were considered a human rights violation. In 2007, after a $53,000,000 renovation, the luxury hotel became a nightlife hot spot for beautiful, young Bostonians. The lobby and bar were bustling with $3,000 high-heeled shoes and George Q shirts.

    We would return from a hard day on set with our clothes torn, stained, and covered with bear slobber and dirt. Doug worked the hardest, so he always looked the worst. One evening, as the uniformed doorman opened the huge brass doors for us, he looked at Doug and said to me, "You know, Mrs. Seus, if he didn't have a room key, I would think he was a homeless person."

    Five-star hotel or not, to me the Liberty still felt like an old jail. The granite-walled fortress was confining, and a sense of sadness tapped me on the shoulder. Our room was a converted cell; one wall was exposed 19th-century brick. The only window, which could not be opened, looked out on the emergency room entrance of Massachusetts General Hospital. The sound of sirens replaced the songs of chickadees and warblers outside my bedroom window at home. I was never quite so glad to get out of a place in my life.

After two months in "jail," Jed and I drove Tank back to Utah. When we crossed to the west side of the Missouri River, we rolled the windows all the way down and blasted John Denver's "I'd Rather Be a Cowboy" as loud as we could.

~~~~~~~~~~~~~~~~~~~~~~~~

We Bought a Zoo

Not long after the *Zookeeper*, another script with lions and tigers and bears (oh my!) came our way. We thought maybe we should pass, but it was such a beautiful story, a film adaptation of Benjamin Mee's memoir, *We Bought a Zoo*, starring Matt Damon and Scarlett Johansen, and directed by the extraordinary Cameron Crowe. Benjamin Mee, played by Matt Damon, is deeply grieving the loss of his wife. His 14-year-old son, acting out his pain and anger at the loss of his mother, is expelled from school. The young family needs to heal and starts looking for a home in the country that will provide a fresh start. Finally, the perfect house presents itself but there is one problem: it comes with a dilapidated but fully populated zoo that has been closed to the public for several years. The family struggles to reopen the shabby zoo under the watchful eye of the film's antagonist, a strict USDA inspector.

The bear in the story is named Buster, a sad and depressed creature who one day escapes from the crumbling zoo and wanders the streets of the nearby town. Benjamin, who just happens to be in town on errands, discovers the escape when he comes to a stop sign and Buster walks calmly in front of his car. Buster turns, pokes his nose against the driver's side window, pushes on it, and moves on. (Matt and Bart were nose-to-nose in the shot.) Benjamin calls the zoo crew together, and all rush to recapture Buster before his escape becomes known and ruins the zoo.

Benjamin is the first to find the bear, who is joyfully celebrating his freedom in a meadow. He approaches, gun loosely in hand, trying to sweet-talk Buster back to the zoo. Buster walks deliberately toward him. Benjamin announces, "Buster, this is a big gun, and I don't want to shoot you." Buster spares Mee that painful decision by swatting the gun away — far away. Actually, it was Jed who doubled Matt in that scene, which landed him in the Screen Actors Guild like his sister. Buster then approaches so close that his roar sprays slobber into Benjamin's face. The bear could kill him. Instead, they share a few seconds of deep understanding, brilliantly captured by director Cameron Crowe.

Just as the bear lowers his head, *pop*, he is tranquilized by a zookeeper and Bart gets to perform his famous "dying bear act." As the dart gunner explains to Benjamin how close he had come to becoming "chips and salsa," Benjamin announces, "I saw him up here on the hill, by himself, utterly free … I want to make his enclosure bigger … much bigger." Aside from the beautiful story about the small zoo, the film tells several heartwarming stories about life, love, and overcoming loss.

We reminisced with Matt about sitting behind him and Ben

Matt Damon unexpectedly finds "Buster" the escaped zoo bear, played by Bart the Bear 2.

Affleck at the 1998 Oscars, when Bart had held the envelope before Matt and Ben won the Oscar for *Good Will Hunting*, and the moment that Matt let us hold his Oscar. We spoke of our shared passion and concern for the planet. His calling was to work for clean water, a rare and precious treasure in many places. He talked about seeing the faces of his own children on those of the 2 million children that die each year for lack of clean water. Our fervor for caring for the earth fit together as pieces of a puzzle. How priceless is a sparkling-clean mountain stream flowing through an undisturbed forest?

~~~~~~~~~~~~~~~~~~~~~~~

Game of Thrones

For weeks, our good man Smitty, all 6 feet 4 inches of him, pranced around our yard in a sassy blond wig and falsies that added nice curves under the full-length dress. Our conservative neighbors sent more than a few curious glances our way. We were perversely quiet and offered no explanation for Smitty's sudden gender transformation.

It was 2013, and emails had long since replaced phone calls; there had been a query from Bernadette Caulfield, the executive producer for the hit series *Game of Thrones*. She shared that there was an upcoming episode, "The Bear and the Maiden Fair." In it, the evil Lord has captured Brienne of Tarth, played by Gwendoline Christy. She is thrown into a deep, wooden pit with a huge, ferocious bear. They give her a sword, but alas, it is made of wood. Galloping over the hills, Jamie Lannister, played by Nikolaj Coster-Waldau, comes to the rescue and hoists her out of the pit as the bear bites and claws at his legs. Smitty was the perfect stunt double for the beautiful, tall, and slender Gwendoline (well, maybe not the beautiful part). Doug was the same height and size as Nikolaj.

It seemed too good to be true, except for a logistic lunacy —

Bart the Bear 2 in the pit with Nikolaj Coster-Waldau and Gwendoline Christy for *Game of Thrones*.

Game of Thrones was being filmed in Belfast, Ireland. Yes, we had taken Big Bart to Austria and Little Bart to New Zealand without a hitch, but those destinations were equipped to handle jumbo jets — no such luck in Belfast. There was a way to get Bart to Belfast, but it would have required we drive to Los Angeles, take a jumbo jet to Frankfurt, transfer the trailer to a one-ton army truck and drive from Germany across Belgium to Calais in the north of France, take the Chunnel to Kent Downs in England, drive across England (through London) to Liverpool, load the truck and trailer onto a ferry, and cross the Irish Sea to Belfast in Northern Ireland. That would have meant five international border crossings for Bart with the documentation required by each country, along with the "passport papers" required by the Convention on International Trade in Endangered Species.

The journey would have taken two weeks. Obviously, there was no way we would put Bart through such an odyssey. He would have enjoyed the cool and quiet white noise of the transatlantic airplane ride, but the rest would have been a nightmare for him. However, the executive producer knew what she wanted for the epic episode and would settle for no less than Bart. So, she would bring the entire cast and crew to the United States. We would film at Santa Clarita Studios, a few miles north of Los Angeles, where they would reconstruct the Game of Thrones set. The director was Michelle McClearn, a tiny bundle of dynamite who knew how to explode the screen.

Our shooting dates were scheduled for early February, so one dark January afternoon we snuggled up to Bart, who was curled up in his den of sweet hay, and asked, "How would you like to go south for a bit?" Not long after, the *Game of Thrones* wardrobe department sent us a package that included the pink velvet dress for Smitty, and medieval jerkins for Doug, along with a wooden sword.

Gwendoline and Nikolaj did their own scenes with Bart in the pit, but for the hits, mauls, bites, and claws — they were doubled by Smitty and Doug. Since it was winter, Bart's appetite was still a bit sleepy, but he loved the spotlight and responded to the energy of applause and praise far beyond the reward of cookies. The set sounded like the Super Bowl when the big beast showed off for the spectators. I don't know what it was about the cast and crew, perhaps the humor of the British people, but not since *Without a Paddle* had we had so much fun on a set.

Epilogue

"You Can't Do That!"

It is late autumn. A blizzard of ochre-colored cottonwood leaves whirls a spirit dance over the bears' pond. They are shaped like bird feathers and fly away in masses like a great eagle heading south.

Today it is Tank's turn in the pond. He seems to understand the dance of the leaves as he lifts himself from the pond and shakes the water from his new winter coat. Clusters of crystals spin in a circle around his head in the bright southern sunlight. He comes to sit beside me for a moment. He leans on my shoulder, wet and cold. I love it. He smells so clean, like a forest after a rain. The sun sneaks behind the ridge of the foothill that has been our closest neighbor for over 40 years. Tank toddles off to his den, and I head for the house.

The front door opens beside my desk. Its old oak top is covered ... a new screenplay and a storyboard for a commercial featuring Bart as "Fluffy" the family pet of a lumberjack's family; a thank-you note from the BBC praising Bart's work in a special that will be seen worldwide; most importantly, the latest newsletter from Vital Ground announcing the newest additions to the nearly one million acres of wildlands the organization has conserved — one landscape, for bears and people.

"You can't do this," they had said. Well, we did. We achieved our preposterous dream.

Never doubt yourself. Work until your back aches, stumble, be humiliated, square your shoulders, start over, and do it again. If you don't believe in yourself, who will? If you don't try, you won't know.

The apple tree on Bart the Bear's grave grows strong. It blooms every Spring.

Time of the Lilacs — 50 Years Later

The window is open to the new spring air. The seed-filled catkins hang from the Aspen tree like Christmas ornaments. We planted the tree over 40 years ago when it was only knee-high. Now it towers over the house. Its once smooth white bark is now rough and worn like my hands.

Behind the Aspen is a wall of lavender and purple — the lilac hedge we planted at the same time to shade Big Bart's den. Soon it will be cool and green, but for now, Doug and I touch and smile at each other, remembering the time of lilacs 50 years before. What a journey we have shared with our beloved animals, children, and grandchildren. The wrinkles around our eyes are maps to the places we have been.

Doug and I with Bart the Bear 2, our children, grandchildren, and children's partners in 2018. First, and always first, we were a family.

In Loving Memory

Our son, Clint. March 31, 1963 – August 10, 2010.

Postscript

The closest we ever came to having a pastor was a Navajo elder named Julius Chavez. He would be at our side at a call, no matter the hour — for birth, sickness, celebration, and death. He presided with prayers, songs, eagle wings, sweetgrass, and sage. He was deeply honored by his own people and by all who were touched by his healing, no matter their ethnicity.

Julius Chavez with his ceremonial eagle wings.

Julius was also one of the few male weavers in the Navajo nation. He opened Vital Ground's 20th and 30th anniversaries with prayers and songs in his native tongue. His weavings containing Bart's fur sold for tens of thousands of dollars at Vital Ground auctions, with every cent going to wildlands and wild ones. Only two of those rugs exist on the planet, woven with carded grizzly hair and his mother's hand-spun wool from Navajo Churro sheep.

Each spring, Doug curried Bart's winter coat with combs made for Belgian draft hoses. Bart loved it. Eventually, we would give Julius the fur, a combination of stiff guard hairs and downy undercoat. He would "spin" it by rubbing the fur on his thigh toward his heart, the direction required for sacred use. After many months, there would be grapefruit-sized balls of the amber-colored yarn. In a year, there would be a powerful weaving.

For the first of the cherished rugs, Julius was inspired by the story of Bart's experience with the New Zealand sky. The golden yarn would become the figure of the Great Bear — Ursa Major. In Navajo tradition, stars were woven on his paws to represent the four sacred mountains. Cassiopeia, the Big Dipper, and the North Star graced the border. The rug now hangs in the heart of our home.

Julius' rug, woven with Bart the Bear's fur, depicting Urus Major – Big Bear.

Corn pollen is an important part of many Navajo rituals, so when Julius asked us to cover Bart's neck with pollen to give it the healing power of the bear, we were honored. Julius explained that as a medicine man, the Great Bear — the guardian to the door of the sun — was too powerful for him to be near. For the ceremony, Julius remained in the house and prayed in reverence. Bart was always ready to romp and wrestle with Doug; however, on the day of the pollen ceremony, he sat on his haunches as we approached him with the beaded deerskin medicine bag of pollen. The pollen sparkled in the sun like gold dust on his chocolate-brown fur. He lay on his belly to give us easy reach as we carefully scraped the pollen back into the bag.

The corn pollen, made holy and healing, was taken to the mountains where Julius blessed it with Native prayers and cedar smoke through the night. It was then carried to the reservation, where bundles were given to medicine men. The next day, Julius wrote us: *We continued praying and putting on cedar through the night for all of you. His pollen sure filled a lot of bundles for the reservation. Many medicine men expressed how grateful they were for what we shared with them. Bart's prayers and power for healing continues for generations to come.*

~~~~~~~~~~~~~~~~~~~~~~~~~~

Doug applying the ceremonial corn pollen on Bart the Bear 2.

In the Spring of 2021, Bart began to show signs of illness — his coat turned dull, and he failed to shed. He was listless. We reached out to our zoo vet friends and proceeded with blood draws. Initial results were inconclusive, so we sent the blood to zoos and to fish and game departments in Wyoming, Montana, and Alaska, and we finally got a diagnosis: liver cancer. Only pain and suffering awaited our orphaned cub, our companion, our teacher, our Bart.

When the time had come, we called the vet and Julius. The grave was ready beside Big Bart's beneath the apple tree. The November day dawned bright and clear. Our family held tightly to each other as we stepped outside to say goodbye. We found Bart on his belly, head down, at peace. He had slipped away in the night as if to spare us the final sorrow of administering euthanasia drugs.

As we gently lowered Bart into his earthen cradle, Julius and the other elders sang sacred songs to "grandfather." Our family, children, grandchildren, and close friends laid clothing, blankets, beads, cookies, and special stones over him.

Our dear Julius passed of Covid six weeks after laying Bart to rest. He was buried in a traditional ceremony on the Navajo Nation at Many Farms, Arizona, beside his mother.

All souls, Doug and I too, will pass from this earth. Only a wondrous planet remains. Both of our beloved Barts have helped heal the wounds on this earth, bringing joy to so many and caring for their wild brothers and sisters. A great work carries forth in their name.

Vital Ground

Where the Grizzly can walk, the earth is healthy and whole.
It has to be.
The kingdom of the Great Bear demands true wildness.
Every green growing, winged, creeping or crawling, swimming, four-legged or
two-legged can follow his tracks into the Cathedral of Undisturbed Creation.

Wilderness does not need us, we need wilderness. By being there we are changed.
Wilderness lights the rim fire of our soul. The singing silence will restore sanity.

If all our scriptures, scrolls, dogmas, and demigods were somehow to be
left out in the elements they would be shortly absorbed into the dust of the
earth that bore them. What then would teach us? Would we know what to do?

Can we touch Creation and find God within ourselves to understand this
deep blue hanging ball of rock, fire, and water? Our species has evolved with minds
that have learned to split the atom. With such power can we protect and keep the
few and fragile bits of untouched wilderness in our world?

Where the grizzly can walk, the earth is healthy and whole –
And it is holy.

Credits

FEATURE FILMS
1976 *Baker's Hawk*, Doty-Dayton Productions
1978 *Strange Force on Thunder Mountain*, American National Entertainment
1979 *Wind River*, Columbia Pictures
1980 *Across the Great Divide*, Pacific International Enterprises, Santa Fe International
1980 *Windwalker*, Pacific International Enterprises
1981 *Surroundvision*, Disney WED Enterprises
1982 *Grand Canyon: Rivers of Time* (Imax), Destination Cinema
1983 *The Beast*, Frameline Productions
1983 *In Search of a Golden Sky*, Com World
1983 *The Gambler: The Adventure Continues*, Lion Share
1984 *The Journey of Natty Gann*, Walt Disney Studios
1985 *Clan of the Cave Bear*, Warner Brothers
1985 *Classics Illustrated*, Sunn Classic Pictures
1987 *The Bear*, Tri-Star / Renn Productions
1988 *The Great Outdoors*, Universal Studios
1990 *Waiting for Salazar*, Bitteroot Productions
1990 *On Deadly Ground*, Warner Brothers
1991 *Lost in the Barrens*, Canadian Broadcasting Company
1991 *Indian Runner*, Indian River Production
1991 *White Fang*, Walt Disney Studios
1992 *Stay Tuned*, Morgan Creek Entertainment
1993 *Wind River*, Doty-Daton Productions
1994 *The Giant*, Richard Kiel Productions
1994 *Walking Thunder*, Majestic Enterprises
1994 *Yellowstone* (Imax), Vineyard Productions
1995 *The Great American West* (Imax), Janson Media
1995 *Red River*, Karukeva Productions (French)
1995 *Legends of the Fall*, Tri-Star Pictures
1996 *The Edge*, 20th Century Fox
1997 *Meet the Deedles*, Walt Disney Studios
1999 *Like a Mother Bear*, Crown Sephira Productions
2000 *Lewis and Clark*, Great Journey West (Imax)
2000 *Dr. Dolittle 2*, 20th Century Fox
2003 *Big Fish*, Columbia Pictures
2003 *Unfinished Life*, Miramax
2003 *Without a Paddle*, Paramount
2004 *Into The West*, TNT / Dreamworks

2006 *Evan Almighty*, Universal Pictures
2006 *Into The Wild*, Sean Penn / Paramount
2008 *Horse Crazy*, The Legend of Grizzly Mountain, Medication Productions
2009 *Have you Heard About the Morgans?*, Columbia Pictures
2011 *ZooKeeper*, MGM Studios
2011 *Druid Peak*, Zelnick Mayer Productions
2011 *We Bought a Zoo*, 20th Century Fox
2013 *Red Machine*, Red Machine Canada
2014 *Girl's Camp Movie*, Thrillion Dollar Productions
2015 *Once I Was a Beehive*, Main Dog Productions
2015 *Pete's Dragon*, Walt Disney Studios
2015 *Into the Grizzly Maze*, Indomitable Entertainment
2017 *Radioflash*, American Dream Labs

TELEVISION
1977 *Centennial*, Mitchner Mini Series, NBC
1978 *Deerslayer*, Sunn Classic Pictures
1978 *Grizzly Adams*, Sunn Classic Pictures
1979 *Lobo, King of the Currumpau*, Canadian Broadcasting Company
1979 *National Wildlife Foundation*, Cine Designs Films
1980 *Mr. Kruger's Christmas*, Bonneville Productions
1980 *The Predators*, National Geographic TV (Produced by Wasatch Rocky Mt. Wildlife)
1981 *Camping in Bear Country*, U.S. Forest Service
1982 *Wild America*, PBS
1982 *The Man Who Loved Bears*, PBS
1982 *Black Bears*, BBC
1986 *Down the Long Hills*, Walt Disney Studios
1989 Today Show, NBC
1990 *The Aldo Leopold Story*, Florentine Films
1990 *The Young Riders* "The Decoy," MGM (Bart the Bear Guest Star)
1990 *Entertainment Tonight*, NBC
1990 *Radiotelevisione Italiana* (RAI)
1990 *Those Amazing Animals*, CBS
1991 *Lifestyles of the Rich & Famous*, NBC
1991 *The Today Show*, NBC
1992 *Cross Roads* "Amanda," R. Yuric Riders Productions
1994 *McKenna* "Bear," A.K.A. Productions
1995 *Entertainment Tonight*, ABC
1996 *Inside Edition*, CBS
1996 *Jack Hanna Animal Adventures*, Hanna Productions
1996 *Lonesome Dove*, Motown Productions
1996 *Deadman's Walk*, RHI Productions

1997 *Stray Dog*, Lynch Entertainment / Nickelodeon
1998 *70th Academy Awards Ceremony*, Gil Cates Production
  (Bart, special presenter)
1999 *Ballad of Lucy Whipple*, Movie of the Week, CAP Production
1999 *Animal Smarts*, 48 Hours CBS
2000 *Bart the Bear*, 48 Hours CBS
2000 *Christmas in the Clouds*, Unapix Productions
2001 *The Tonight Show with Jay Leno*, NBC
2002 *Everwood*, Warner Brothers TV
2002 *Olympic Feature*, International Sports Broadcasting
2003 *Entertainment Tonight*, NBC
2003 *Oprah Winfrey*, ABC
2003 *Access Hollywood*, ABC
2004 *Mr. Sirura's Zoo*, Nipon Television
2005 *CSI*, CBS
2005 *Everwood*, Warner Brothers TV
2005 *The Amazing Race*, CBS
2006 *National Geographic Explorer*, National Geographic TV
2007 *On the Lot*, Dreamworks, NBC
2012 *60 Minutes Australia*, www.9news.com/
2013 *Game of Thrones*, season 3, episode 7, HBO
2014 *Good Morning America*, ABC News
2014 *Nightline*, ABC News
2014 State of Alaska Dept. of Tourism Campaign
2015 *Tairiku Oudan Adventure*, Dragon Entertainment
2016 *Red Bull Performing Under Pressure*, Red Bull High Performance
2019 *Man Vs. Bear*, Discovery Channel

DOCUMENTARIES
1987 *The Grizzlies*, National Geographic Society
1988 *Grizzly and Man, an Uneasy Truce*, National Audubon Society
1995 *River of Bears*, Komo TV
1996 *Wild on the Set*, Discovery
1997 *Ordinary Extraordinary*, NBC
1997 *The Baddest Bear*, National Geographic TV
1997 *Animal Minds*, Nova
1997 *Bearly Acting*, CNN Impact
1997 *Movie Magic*, Glacier Point Productions
1998 *How'd They Do That?*, Time Warner
1998 *Bart the Bear*, Stories Unlimited, German Television
1998 *Lights, Camera, BEARS*, National Geographic TV
2001 *Wild on the Set*, Discovery Channel

2001 *Growing Up Grizzly*, Animal Planet Channel
2002 *Vets*, Discovery Channel, Manitou Motion Pictures
2003 *Growing Up Grizzly 2*, Arden Entertainment
2007 *Lobo, the Wolf That Changed America*, BBC and WNET
2021 *Animal Emperor*, BBC

COMMERCIALS
1979 Coors Beer, Denny Harris of California Productions
1979 Busch Beer, EUE Screen Gems
1981 U.S. Postal Service, David Quaid Productions
1982 Sergio Valenti Jeans, Benard Hirshenson
1982 Toyota, Fred Levinson / NY Productions, Superbowl Commercial
1982 Levis, Go West Productions
1985 Nissan, Fred Levinson Productions
1985 Scott Towels, Jon Yarbourgh & Co
1986 Kodiak Smokeless Tobacco, Dick Clintsman Productions
1989 Levis, Plum Productions
1989 U.S. Postal Service, Ian Leech/Marol Buthuer
1989 Chevron, EVE Screen Gems
1990 Amstel Beer, Miller Osmond Productions
1991 La Batts Beer, Rick Levine Productions
1991 Bayer Aspirin, Plum Productions
1992 Old Milwaukee Beer, Propaganda Films
1993 Jelly Juice, CPG Productions, Japan
1995 Marlboro, Plum Productions
1995 Pursuit Herbicide, Sutterholm Productions
1999 Animal Cancer Center, Colorado State University
2000 Marlboro, Steven, Weill Productions
2000 Cell Phone, Austria Productions
2005 Nikon Camera, National Geographic Image Sales
2007 P.S.A. for Vital Ground, Zooprax Productions
2007 Volkswagen Bus, Brooks Freehill Images
2007 Direct TV, Impatient Cow Productions
2008 Tums, Arnolds of New York / Anonymous Content Productions
2009 Master Card, Anonymous Content Productions
2011 Verizon, Harvest Film
2014 Young Living Essential Oils, Young Living Productions
2015 Nokia, Freakin' Rad Productions
2016 Red Bull Performing Under Pressure
2017 Kodiak Cakes, Kodiak Cakes, LLC
2020 Kodiak Cakes, Kodiak Cakes, LLC
2020 Teton Sports

2021 Built Bar
2021 Kodiak Cakes, Kodiak Cakes, LLC
2022 Dell Computer Sawtooth Rugged
2022 Kodiak Cakes, Kodiak Cakes, LLC

PRINT PUBLICATIONS
1982 Dec, LIFE Magazine, Feature story
1984 Aug, LIFE Magazine, Cover
1986 Feb, National Geographic, Feature story
1987 Jan, Backpacker Magazine, Feature story
1989 Nov, People Magazine, Inside spread feature
1989 Spring, LIFE Magazine, Special Hollywood Issue
1990 Jan, People Weekly, Featured Story
1991 July, Boy's Life, Featured Story
1992 Mar, National Geographic World, Inside spread feature
1993 Summer, Outside Magazine, Featured story
1993 June, Architectural Digest, Feature story
1993 Aug, Backpacker Magazine, Article
1995 Nov, Outside Magazine, Cover
1996 Sept, Men's Health Magazine, Featured story
1997 Sept, TIME Magazine, Featured review
1997 Sept, Sports Afield, Cover
1997 Sept, News Week, Featured Review
1999 May, National Geographic World, Featured story
1999 May, LIFE Magazine, Commemorative Issue
2001 Jun, National Geographic, Featured story
2001 July, People Magazine, Featured review
2002 Jan, National Geographic, Cover
2003 Jan, National Geographic Kids, Featured story
2015 Hobo Magazine (Paris, France), Featured story
2020 March, Empire Magazine, Featured story
2020 May, Men's Journal, Featured story

www.ingramcontent.com/pod-product-compliance
Lightning Source LLC
Chambersburg PA
CBHW052128030426
42337CB00028B/5069